MW01444517

THE GEOPOLITICS OF ISRAEL AND THE PALESTINIANS

The Intelligence Behind the Headlines

STRATFOR
GLOBAL INTELLIGENCE

STRATFOR
700 Lavaca Street, Suite 900
Austin, Texas 78701

Copyright © 2009 by STRATFOR
All rights reserved, including the right of reproduction in whole or in part

Printed in the United States of America

The contents of this book originally appeared as analyses on STRATFOR's *subscription Web site.*

ISBN: 1448668824
EAN-13: 9781448668823

CONTENTS

Introduction	1
1. The Importance of Place	7
2. Groundwork	54
3. Turning Points	69
4. Breaking Points	96
5. Israeli Decisions and the Broader World	122
6. A Giant Sucking Sound	147

INTRODUCTION

The Arab-Israeli conflict and its immediate subset, the Israeli-Palestinian conflict, are normally approached in moral terms. When the case for a Jewish state is juxtaposed with the rights of the Palestinians an infinite regression takes place, one in which each side makes a moral claim for its rights based on historical claims and demonstrations of historical wrongs.

In a certain sense the moral argument is irrelevant, simply because neither side is going to be convinced of the error of its position, certainly not to the point of abandoning its historical claims or no longer pursuing its political interests. This is not unique to the Israeli-Palestinian situation — it is a universal condition. Americans or Australians are not about to abandon their homes and return to where they or their ancestors came from because of the strength of a moral argument. Poland is not going to regain its historical borders through moral suasion. Morality is not completely irrelevant, of course, but it is not the strength of the moral argument that determines the outcome of the dispute.

The Arab-Israeli and Israeli-Palestinian conflicts are rooted in the rise of modern nationalism after the French Revolution. The principle of the revolution was the doctrine of national self-determination. Behind this was the idea that each nation — as it was defined linguistically, historically, culturally and, above all, geographically — had the right to determine its own course within its own boundaries. As the great dynastic empires declined, these nations represented the residue, what was left after the empires were boiled away. Europe proliferated with nations seeking to determine their own destiny.

In part this was a moral enterprise. In part it was simply survival. In a world of nation-states, a nation without a state was a victim, a mere ethnic group at risk of succumbing to the will of the majority. It followed that every nation that had the power to assert its nationalism did so in the 19th and 20th centuries.

The Jews were in a peculiar position. They were a people without a clear geography. The majority of Jews, particularly in Western Europe, gravitated to the view that they were simply a religion, not a nation. It followed that they could have been of any nationality, as Christians were. When the Zionist movement began to develop in the late 19th century, it was a response to European theories of nationalism more than to any religious sense of nation. The founders of Zionism saw the Jews as a nation among other nations, looking for a geography of their own. The Western European Zionists were in the minority among Jews, to say the least.

The situation was different in the Russian empire. There, the idea that Judaism was simply a religion and that Jews were citizens of Russia was explicitly rejected by the state, which saw them as a distinct, non-Russian entity, ultimately alien. This is where Zionism took root. With the shift in Russian policy in the 1880s, many Russian Jews were forced out of Russia. Most came to the United States. Some, however, wanted to create a Jewish state in the only area that they could claim through historical right — Palestine.

The merger of the theory of national rights with the reality of the Russian Jews created the first real Zionist movement. The holocaust simply created another mass of Jews without a home who believed that without a homeland another holocaust was inevitable. The holocaust also forced a change in mindset upon European Jews who had previously rejected Zionism because they saw themselves as not particularly atypical when compared to other Europeans. Now they were forced to see themselves -- and the Zionist movement -- in a starkly different light.

Palestinian nationalism also was rooted in the European notion of the nation-state, but in a more complex way. The Ottoman Empire, like the Russian, was a multi-national empire dominated by Turks. The Arabs, particularly in the Arabian Peninsula and Levant, were subjects of the Ottomans and in their minds victims. This had been a long-standing reality, but it was transformed by the British Empire.

During World War I, the Turks were allied with the Germans and Austro-Hungarians against the British, French and Russians. The British wished to generate an uprising in the Arabian Peninsula in order to secure Arabia, drive north toward Damascus via Palestine, and ultimately force Ottoman troops to fight in the Middle East rather than in Europe or Russia. In order to do this the British formed alliances with Bedouin tribes in Arabia, seeking to unite them under the principle of Arab (as opposed to Muslim) nationalism. The British took an ethnic identity, Arab, and tried to turn it into a nation. They succeeded militarily and politically. The British laid the foundation for an idea that had been present in the Arab world since the French conquered Egypt under Napoleon — the idea of an Arab nation.

Over time, this doctrine evolved into the idea of pan-Arabism under Gamel Abdul Nasser after he seized power in Egypt in the early 1950s. By then Israel had come into existence, opposed by Muslim states under the doctrine that the Jews had seized land that had historically belonged to Muslims. Nasser radicalized this by arguing that it was not a religious issue but a national one — that the Jews had taken the land from the Arab nation. At first, the Arab nation, not the Palestinians, were the claimants to the land.

However, under Nasser, the Palestine Liberation Organization was created. It was not clear that its mission was the creation of an independent Palestine state, or that it was an organization of Arabs from Palestine seeking to liberate Arab Palestine. There was, as we shall see, ambiguity at first. But inevitably the claims of the inhabitants of Palestine to their homeland were transformed into a claim for a Palestinian state.

In a real sense, the origin of the modern variants of both Jewish and Palestinian nationalism was rooted in the struggle of the British against the Ottomans. Seizing every tool possible, the British both generated Arab nationalism and endorsed Jewish nationalism, issuing the Balfour Declaration in 1917, which affirmed the Jewish right to a homeland in an area not under British authority at the time. A year earlier, the British had promised Sharif Hussein, the leader of Mecca, kingship over all of Arabia. The irony of this is interesting, but hardly critical. Treaties and moral claims are generated like electricity during wars and the British did what they had to do to win.

They left a general conundrum, however. Palestine was seen by the Jews as both their historical homeland and a guarantee by the British, who later controlled the land under a mandate by the League of Nations. The Palestinians saw Palestine as the location of their homes and a right guaranteed by the British in their support of the Arab nation.

The world is constantly waiting for Jews and Palestinians to reach a compromise on this issue. They always assume that the problem is stubbornness. What follows is an attempt to explain the intractability of the Israeli-Palestinian conflict in the context of the Arab-Israeli conflict. We begin by presenting two monographs, one on Israeli geopolitics and the other on Palestinian geopolitics. Following this there is a sampling of analyses written by STRATFOR over the past 10 years or so chronicling the evolution of the region during that time.

This is far from the definitive book on the subject. But it is designed to offer an introduction to a geopolitical approach to the Israeli-Palestinian conflict and to explain some of the underlying issues and tensions. We offer no solution other than the observation that no solution is possible without a clear and dispassionate understanding of the problem.

Devising a solution depends on power, which in turn depends on the interactions of people, politics and geography. And perhaps nowhere can the decisive nature of geopolitics be more clearly seen than in Israel, the West Bank and the Gaza Strip.

STRATFOR
Austin, Texas
Aug. 1, 2009

CHAPTER 1: The Importance of Place

The Geopolitics of Israel
May 4, 2008

The founding principle of geopolitics is that place — geography — plays a significant role in determining how nations will behave. If that theory is true, then there ought to be a deep continuity in a nation's foreign policy. Israel is a laboratory for this theory, since it has existed in three different manifestations in roughly the same place, twice in antiquity and once in modernity. If geopolitics is correct, then Israeli foreign policy, independent of policymakers, technology or the identity of neighbors, ought to have important common features. This is, therefore, a discussion of common principles in Israeli foreign policy over nearly 3,000 years.

For convenience, we will use the term "Israel" to connote all of the Hebrew and Jewish entities that have existed in the Levant since the invasion of the region as chronicled in the Book of Joshua. As always, geopolitics requires a consideration of three dimensions: the internal geopolitics of Israel, the interaction of Israel and the immediate neighbors who share borders with it, and Israel's interaction with what we will call great powers, beyond Israel's borderlands.

Israel has manifested itself three times in history. The first manifestation began with the invasion led by Joshua and lasted through its division into two kingdoms, the Babylonian conquest of the Kingdom of Judah and the deportation to Babylon early in the sixth century B.C. The second manifestation began when Israel was recreated in 540 B.C. by the Persians, who had defeated the Babylonians. The nature of this second manifestation changed in the fourth century B.C., when Greece overran the Persian Empire and Israel, and again in the first century B.C., when the Romans conquered the region.

The second manifestation saw Israel as a small actor within the framework of larger imperial powers, a situation that lasted until the destruction of the Jewish vassal state by the Romans.

Israel's third manifestation began in 1948, following (as in the other cases) an ingathering of at least some of the Jews who had been dispersed after conquests. Israel's founding takes place in the context of the decline and fall of the British Empire and must, at least in part, be understood as part of British imperial history.

During its first 50 years, Israel plays a pivotal role in the confrontation of the United States and the Soviet Union and, in some senses, is hostage to the dynamics of these two countries. In other words, like the first two manifestations of Israel, the third finds Israel continually struggling among independence, internal tension and imperial ambition.

THE IMPORTANCE OF PLACE

1200 B.C.

Israeli Geography and Borderlands

At its height, under King David, Israel extended from the Sinai to the Euphrates, encompassing Damascus. It occupied some, but relatively little, of the coastal region, an area beginning at what today is Haifa and running south to Jaffa, just north of today's Tel Aviv. The coastal area to the north was held by Phoenicia, the area to the south by Philistines. It is essential to understand that Israel's size and shape shifted over time. For example, Judah under the Hasmoneans did not include the Negev but did include the Golan. The general locale of Israel is fixed. Its precise borders have never been.

Thus, it is perhaps better to begin with what never was part of Israel. Israel never included the Sinai Peninsula. Along the coast, it never stretched much farther north than the Litani River in today's Lebanon. Apart from David's extreme extension (and fairly tenuous control) to the north, Israel's territory never stretched as far as Damascus, although it frequently held the Golan Heights. Israel extended many times to both sides of the Jordan but never deep into the Jordanian Desert. It never extended southeast into the Arabian Peninsula.

Israel consists generally of three parts. First, it always has had the northern hill region, stretching from the foothills of Mount Hermon south to Jerusalem. Second, it always contains some of the coastal plain from today's Tel Aviv north to Haifa. Third, it occupies area between Jerusalem and the Jordan River — today's West Bank. At times, it controls all or part of the Negev, including the coastal region between the Sinai to the Tel Aviv area. It may be larger than this at

THE IMPORTANCE OF PLACE

SECOND MANIFESTATION

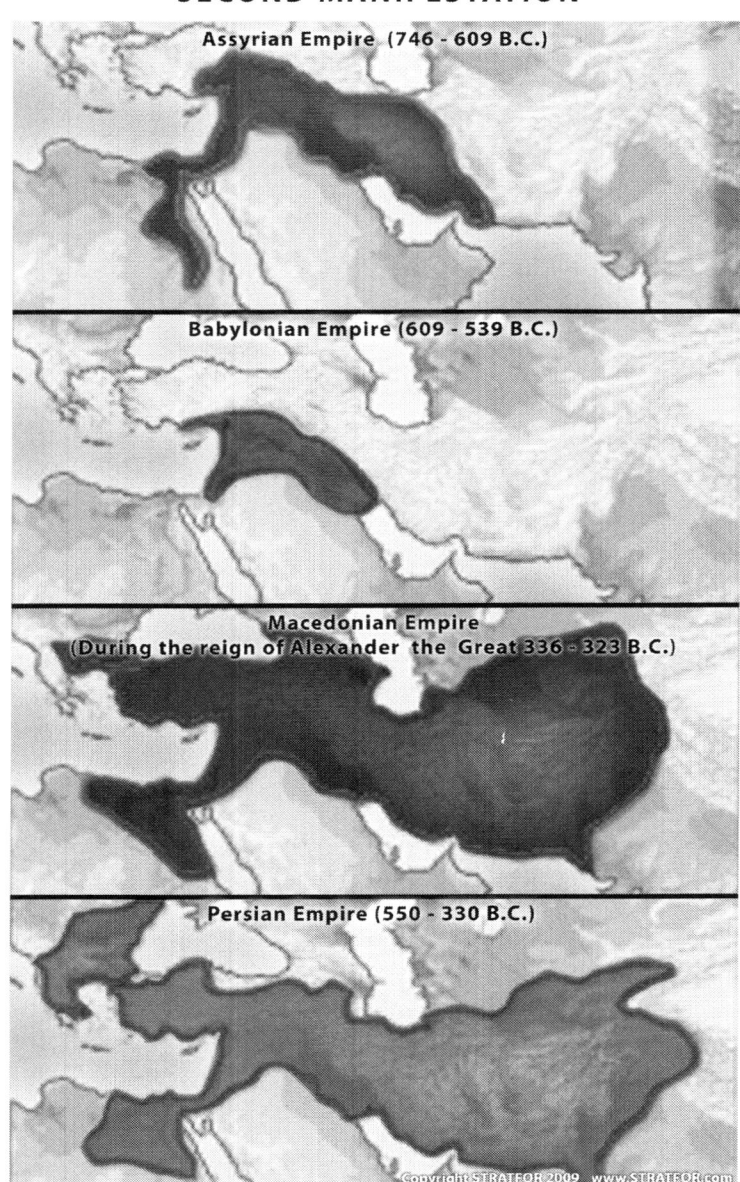

Assyrian Empire (746 - 609 B.C.)

Babylonian Empire (609 - 539 B.C.)

Macedonian Empire
(During the reign of Alexander the Great 336 - 323 B.C.)

Persian Empire (550 - 330 B.C.)

various times in history, and sometimes smaller, but it normally holds all or part of these three regions.

Israel is well-buffered in three directions. The Sinai Desert protects it against the Egyptians. In general, the Sinai has held little attraction for the Egyptians. The difficulty of deploying forces in the eastern Sinai poses severe logistical problems for them, particularly during a prolonged presence. Unless Egypt can rapidly move through the Sinai north into the coastal plain, where it can sustain its forces more readily, deploying in the Sinai is difficult and unrewarding. Therefore, so long as Israel is not so weak as to make an attack on the coastal plain a viable option, or unless Egypt is motivated by an outside imperial power, Israel does not face a threat from the southwest.

Israel is similarly protected from the southeast. The deserts southeast of Eilat-Aqaba are virtually impassable. No large force could approach from that direction, although smaller raiding parties could. The tribes of the Arabian Peninsula lack the reach or the size to pose a threat to Israel, unless massed and aligned with other forces. Even then, the approach from the southeast is not one that they are likely to take. The Negev is secure from that direction.

The eastern approaches are similarly secured by desert, which begins about 20 to 30 miles east of the Jordan River. While indigenous forces exist in the borderland east of the Jordan, they lack the numbers to be able to penetrate decisively west of the Jordan.

Indeed, the normal model is that, so long as Israel controls Judea and Samaria (the modern-day West Bank), then the East Bank of the Jordan River is under the political and sometimes military domination of Israel — sometimes

THE IMPORTANCE OF PLACE

THIRD MANIFESTATION (1948)

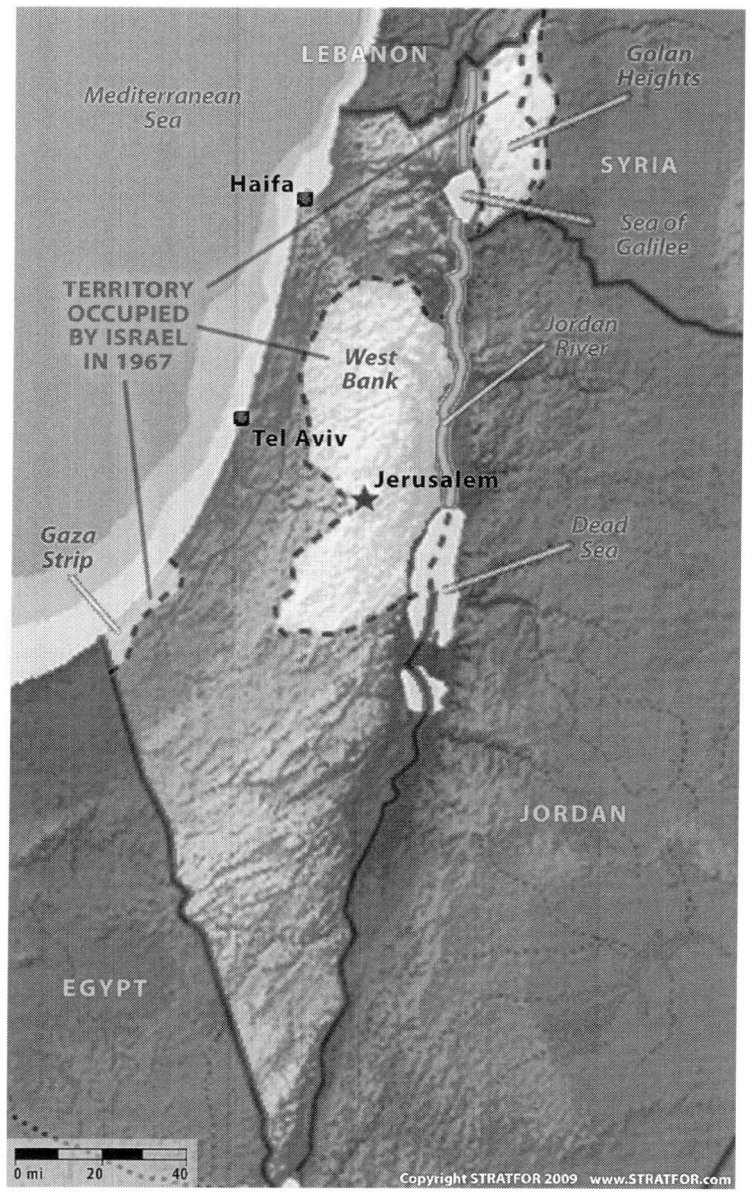

directly through settlement, sometimes indirectly through political influence, or economic or security leverage.

Israel's vulnerability is in the north. There is no natural buffer between Phoenicia and its successor entities (today's Lebanon) to the direct north. The best defense line for Israel in the north is the Litani River, but this is not an insurmountable boundary under any circumstance. However, the area along the coast north of Israel does not present a serious threat. The coastal area prospers through trade in the Mediterranean basin. It is oriented toward the sea and to the trade routes to the east, not to the south. If it does anything, this area protects those trade routes and has no appetite for a conflict that might disrupt trade. It stays out of Israel's way, for the most part.

Moreover, as a commercial area, this region is generally wealthy, a factor that increases predators around it and social conflict within. It is an area prone to instability. Israel frequently tries to extend its influence northward for commercial reasons, as one of the predators, and this can entangle Israel in its regional politics. But barring this self-induced problem, the threat to Israel from the north is minimal, despite the absence of natural boundaries and the large population. On occasion, there is spillover of conflicts from the north, but not to a degree that might threaten regime survival in Israel.

The neighbor that is always a threat lies to the northeast. Syria — or, more precisely, the area governed by Damascus at any time — is populous and frequently has no direct outlet to the sea. It is, therefore, generally poor. The area to its north, Asia Minor, is heavily mountainous. Syria cannot project power to the north except with great difficulty, but powers in Asia Minor can move south. Syria's eastern flank is buffered by a desert that stretches to the Euphrates. Therefore, when there is no threat from the north, Syria's interest — after securing itself internally — is to gain access to the coast. Its primary channel is directly westward, toward the rich cities of the northern Levantine coast, with which it trades heavily. An alternative interest is southwestward, toward the southern Levantine coast controlled by Israel.

As can be seen, Syria can be interested in Israel only selectively. When it is interested, it has a serious battle problem. To attack Israel, it would have to strike between Mount Hermon and the Sea of Galilee, an area about 25 miles wide. The Syrians potentially can attack south of the sea, but only if they are prepared to fight through this region and then attack on extended supply lines. If an attack is mounted along the main route, Syrian forces must descend the Golan Heights and then fight through the hilly Galilee before reaching the coastal plain — sometimes with guerrillas holding out in the Galilean hills. The Galilee is an area that is relatively easy to defend and difficult to attack. Therefore, it is only once Syria takes the Galilee, and can control its lines of supply against guerrilla attack, that its real battle begins.

To reach the coast or move toward Jerusalem, Syria must fight through a plain in front of a line of low hills. This is the decisive battleground where massed Israeli forces, close to lines of supply, can defend against dispersed Syrian forces on extended lines of supply. It is no accident that Megiddo — or Armageddon, as the plain is sometimes referred to — has apocalyptic meaning. This is the point at

THE GEOPOLITICS OF ISRAEL AND THE PALESTINIANS

ISRAEL'S GEOGRAPHY AND BORDERLANDS

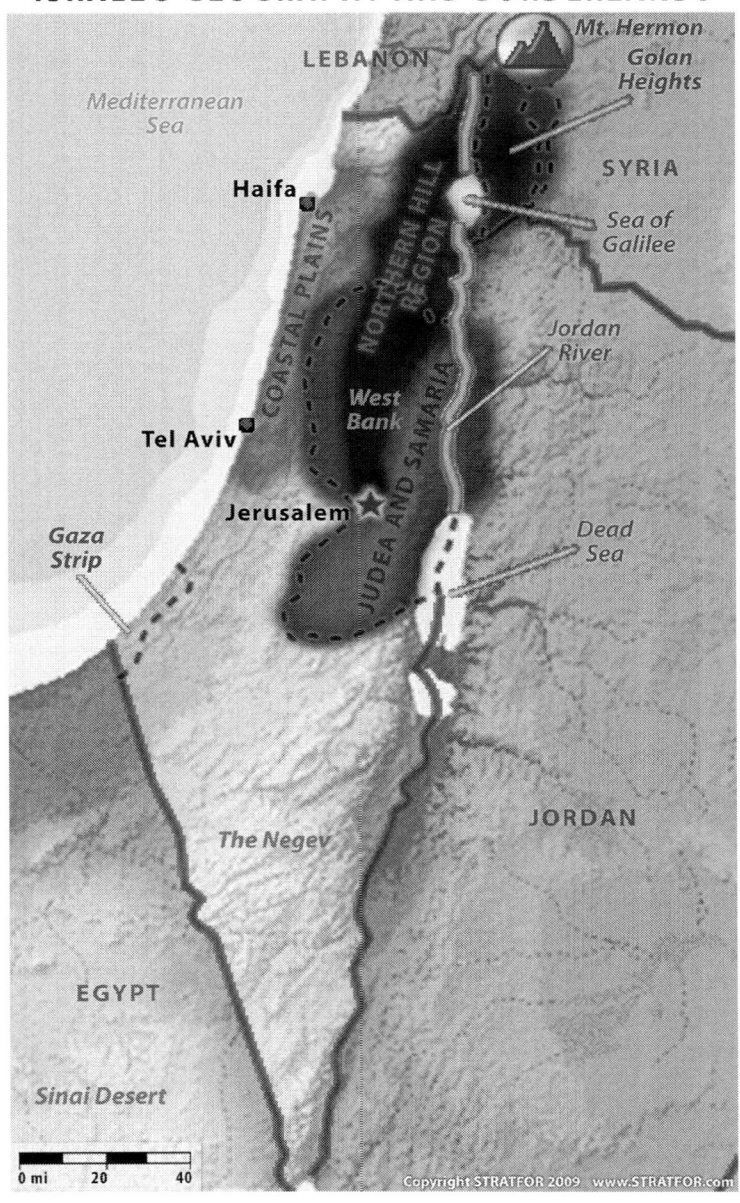

which any move from Syria would be decided. But a Syrian offensive would have a tough fight to reach Megiddo, and a tougher one as it deploys on the plain.

On the surface, Israel lacks strategic depth, but this is true only on the surface. It faces limited threats from southern neighbors. To its east, it faces only a narrow strip of populated area east of the Jordan. To the north, there is a maritime commercial entity. Syria operating alone, forced through the narrow gap of the Mount Hermon-Galilee line and operating on extended supply lines, can be dealt with readily.

There is a risk of simultaneous attacks from multiple directions. Depending on the forces deployed and the degree of coordination between them, this can pose a problem for Israel. However, even here the Israelis have the tremendous advantage of fighting on interior lines. Egypt and Syria, fighting on external lines (and widely separated fronts), would have enormous difficulty transferring forces from one front to another. Israel, on interior lines (fronts close to each other with good transportation), would be able to move its forces from front to front rapidly, allowing for sequential engagement and thereby the defeat of enemies. Unless enemies are carefully coordinated and initiate war simultaneously — and deploy substantially superior force on at least one front — Israel can initiate war at a time of its choosing or else move its forces rapidly between fronts, negating much of the advantage of size that the attackers might have.

There is another aspect to the problem of multifront war. Egypt usually has minimal interests along the Levant, having its own coast and an orientation to the south toward the headwaters of the Nile. On the rare occasions when Egypt does move through the Sinai and attacks to the north and northeast, it is in an expansionary mode. By the time it consolidates and exploits the coastal plain, it would be powerful enough to threaten Syria. From Syria's point of view, the only thing more dangerous than Israel is an Egypt in control of Israel. Therefore, the probability of a coordinated north-south strike at Israel is rare, is rarely coordinated and usually is not designed to be a mortal blow. It is defeated by Israel's strategic advantage of interior lines.

Israeli Geography and the Convergence Zone

Therefore, it is not surprising that Israel's first incarnation lasted as long as it did — some five centuries. What is interesting and what must be considered is why Israel (now considered as the northern kingdom) was defeated by the Assyrians and Judea, then defeated by Babylon. To understand this, we need to consider the broader geography of Israel's location.

Israel is located on the eastern shore of the Mediterranean Sea, on the Levant. As we have seen, when Israel is intact, it will tend to be the dominant power in the Levant. Therefore, Israeli resources must generally be dedicated for land warfare, leaving little over for naval warfare. In general, although Israel had excellent harbors and access to wood for shipbuilding, it never was a major Mediterranean naval power. It never projected power into the sea. The area to the north of Israel has always been a maritime power, but Israel, the area south of Mount Hermon, was always forced to be a land power.

The Levant in general and Israel in particular has always been a magnet for great powers. No Mediterranean empire could be fully secure unless it controlled the Levant. Whether it was Rome or Carthage, a Mediterranean empire that wanted to control both the northern and southern littorals needed to anchor its eastern flank on the Levant. For one thing, without the Levant, a Mediterranean power would be entirely dependent on sea lanes for controlling the other shore. Moving troops solely by sea creates transport limitations and logistical problems. It also leaves imperial lines vulnerable to interdiction — sometimes merely from pirates, a problem that plagued Rome's sea transport. A land bridge, or a land bridge with minimal water crossings that can be easily defended, is a vital supplement to the sea for the movement of large numbers of troops. Once the Hellespont is crossed, the coastal route through southern Turkey, down the Levant and along the Mediterranean's southern shore, provides such an alternative.

There is an additional consideration. If a Mediterranean empire leaves the Levant unoccupied, it opens the door to the possibility of a great power originating to the east seizing the ports of the Levant and challenging the Mediterranean power for maritime domination. In short, control of the Levant binds a Mediterranean empire together while denying a challenger from the east the opportunity to enter the Mediterranean. Holding the Levant, and controlling Israel, is a necessary preventive measure for a Mediterranean empire.

Israel is also important to any empire originating to the east of Israel, either in the Tigris-Euphrates basin or in Persia. For either, security could be assured only once it had an anchor on the Levant. Macedonian expansion under Alexander demonstrated that a power controlling Levantine and Turkish ports could support aggressive operations far to the east, to the Hindu Kush and beyond. While Turkish ports might have sufficed for offensive operations, simply securing the Bosporus still left the southern flank exposed. Therefore, by holding the Levant, an eastern power protected itself against attacks from Mediterranean powers.

The Levant was also important to any empire originating to the north or south of Israel. If Egypt decided to move beyond the Nile Basin and North Africa eastward, it would move first through the Sinai and then northward along the coastal plain, securing sea lanes to Egypt. When Asia Minor powers such as the Ottoman Empire developed, there was a natural tendency to move southward to control the eastern Mediterranean. The Levant is the crossroads of continents, and Israel lies in the path of many imperial ambitions.

Israel therefore occupies what might be called the convergence zone of the Eastern Hemisphere. A European power trying to dominate the Mediterranean or expand eastward, an eastern power trying to dominate the space between the Hindu Kush and the Mediterranean, a North African power moving toward the east, or a northern power moving south — all must converge on the eastern coast of the Mediterranean and therefore on Israel. Of these, the European power and the eastern power must be the most concerned with Israel. For either, there is no choice but to secure it as an anchor.

Internal Geopolitics

Israel is geographically divided into three regions, which traditionally have produced three different types of people. Its coastal plain facilitates commerce, serving as the interface between eastern trade routes and the sea. It is the home of merchants and manufacturers, cosmopolitans — not as cosmopolitan as Phoenicia or Lebanon, but cosmopolitan for Israel. The northeast is hill country, closest to the unruliness north of the Litani River and to the Syrian threat. It breeds farmers and warriors. The area south of Jerusalem is hard desert country, more conducive to herdsman and warriors than anything else. Jerusalem is where these three regions are balanced and governed.

There are obviously deep differences built into Israel's geography and inhabitants, particularly between the herdsmen of the southern deserts and the northern hill dwellers. The coastal dwellers, rich but less warlike than the others, hold the balance or are the prize to be pursued. In the division of the original kingdom between Israel and Judea, we saw the alliance of the coast with the Galilee, while Jerusalem was held by the desert dwellers. The consequence of the division was that Israel in the north ultimately was conquered by Assyrians from the northeast, while Babylon was able to swallow Judea.

Social divisions in Israel obviously do not have to follow geographical lines. However, over time, these divisions must manifest themselves. For example, the coastal plain is inherently more cosmopolitan than the rest of the country. The interests of its inhabitants lie more with trading partners in the Mediterranean and the rest of the world than with their countrymen. Their standard of living is higher, and their commitment to traditions is lower. Therefore, there is an inherent tension between their immediate interests and those of the Galileans, who live more precarious, warlike lives. Countries can be divided over lesser issues — and when Israel is divided it is vulnerable even to regional threats.

We say "even" because geography dictates that regional threats are less menacing than might be expected. The fact that Israel would be outnumbered demographically should all its neighbors turn on it is less important than the fact that it has adequate buffers in most directions, that the ability of neighbors to coordinate an attack is minimal and that their appetite for such an attack is even less. The single threat that Israel faces from the northeast can readily be managed if the Israelis create a united front there. When Israel was overrun by a Damascus-based power, it was deeply divided internally.

It is important to add one consideration to our discussion of buffers, which is diplomacy. The main neighbors of Israel are Egyptians, Syrians and those who live on the east bank of Jordan. This last group is a negligible force demographically, and the interests of the Syrians and Egyptians are widely divergent. Egypt's interests are to the south and west of its territory; the Sinai holds no attraction.

Syria is always threatened from multiple directions, and alliance with Egypt adds little to its security. Therefore, under the worst of circumstances, Egypt and Syria have difficulty supporting each other. Under the best of circumstances, from Israel's point of view, it can reach a political accommodation with Egypt, securing its southwestern frontier politically as well as by geography, thus freeing Israel to concentrate on the northern threats and opportunities.

Israel and the Great Powers

The threat to Israel rarely comes from the region, except when the Israelis are divided internally. The conquests of Israel occur when powers not adjacent to it begin forming empires. Babylon, Persia, Macedonia, Rome, Turkey and Britain all controlled Israel politically, sometimes for worse and sometimes for better. Each dominated it militarily, but none was a neighbor of Israel. This is a consistent pattern. Israel can resist its neighbors; danger arises when more distant powers begin playing imperial games. Empires can bring force to bear that Israel cannot resist.

Israel therefore has this problem: It would be secure if it could confine itself to protecting its interests from neighbors, but it cannot confine itself because its geographic location invariably draws larger, more distant powers toward Israel. Therefore, while Israel's military can focus only on immediate interests, its diplomatic interests must look much further. Israel is constantly entangled with global interests (as the globe is defined at any point), seeking to deflect and align with broader global powers. When it fails in this diplomacy, the consequences can be catastrophic.

Israel exists in three conditions. First, it can be a completely independent state. This condition occurs when there are no major imperial powers external to the region. We might call this the David model. Second, it can live as part of an imperial system — either as a subordinate ally, as a moderately autonomous entity or as a satrapy. In any case, it maintains its identity but loses room for independent maneuvering in foreign policy and potentially in domestic policy. We might call this the Persian model in its most beneficent form. Finally, Israel can be completely crushed — with mass deportations and migrations, with a complete loss of autonomy and minimal residual autonomy. We might call this the Babylonian model.

The Davidic model exists primarily when there is no external imperial power needing control of the Levant that is in a position either to send direct force or to support surrogates in the immediate region. The Persian model exists when Israel aligns itself with the foreign policy interests of such an imperial power, to its own benefit. The Babylonian model exists when Israel miscalculates on the broader balance of power and attempts to resist an emerging hegemon. When we look at Israeli behavior over time, the periods when Israel does not confront hegemonic powers outside the region are not rare, but are far less common than when it is confronting them.

Given the period of the first iteration of Israel, it would be too much to say that the Davidic model rarely comes into play, but certainly since that time, variations of the Persian and Babylonian models have dominated. The reason is geographic. Israel is normally of interest to outside powers because of its strategic position. While Israel can deal with local challenges effectively, it cannot deal with broader challenges. It lacks the economic or military weight to resist. Therefore, it is normally in the process of managing broader threats or collapsing because of them.

The Geopolitics of Contemporary Israel

Let us then turn to the contemporary manifestation of Israel. Israel was recreated because of the interaction between a regional great power, the Ottoman Empire, and a global power, Great Britain. During its expansionary phase, the Ottoman Empire sought to dominate the eastern Mediterranean as well as both its northern and southern coasts. One thrust went through the Balkans toward central Europe. The other was toward Egypt. Inevitably, this required that the Ottomans secure the Levant.

For the British, the focus on the eastern Mediterranean was as the primary sea lane to India. As such, Gibraltar and the Suez were crucial. The importance of the Suez was such that the presence of a hostile, major naval force in the eastern Mediterranean represented a direct threat to British interests. It followed that defeating the Ottoman Empire during World War I and breaking its residual naval power was critical. The British, as was shown at Gallipoli, lacked the resources to break the Ottoman Empire by main force. They resorted to a series of alliances with local forces to undermine the Ottomans. One was an alliance with Bedouin tribes in the Arabian Peninsula; others involved covert agreements with anti-Turkish, Arab interests from the Levant to the Persian Gulf. A third, minor thrust was aligning with Jewish interests globally, particularly those interested in the refounding of Israel. Britain had little interest in this goal, but saw such discussions as part of the process of destabilizing the Ottomans.

The strategy worked. Under an agreement with France, the Ottoman province of Syria was divided into two parts on a line roughly running east-west between the sea and Mount Hermon. The northern part was given to France and divided into Lebanon and a rump Syria entity. The southern part was given to Britain and was called Palestine, after the Ottoman administrative district Philistia. Given the complex politics of the Arabian Peninsula, the British had to find a home for a group of Hashemites, which they located on the east bank of the Jordan River and designated, for want of a better name, the "Trans-Jordan" — the other side of the Jordan. Palestine looked very much like traditional Israel.

The ideological foundations of Zionism are not our concern here, nor are the pre- and post-World War II migrations of Jews, although those are certainly critical. What is important for purposes of this analysis are two things: First, the British emerged economically and militarily crippled from World War II and unable to retain their global empire, Palestine included. Second, the two global powers that emerged after World War II — the United States and the Soviet Union — were engaged in an intense struggle for the eastern Mediterranean after World War II, as can be seen in the Greek and Turkish issues at that time. Neither wanted to see the British Empire survive, each wanted the Levant, and neither was prepared to make a decisive move to take it.

Both the United States and the Soviet Union saw the re-creation of Israel as an opportunity to introduce their power to the Levant. The Soviets thought they might have some influence over Israel due to ideology. The Americans thought they might have some influence given the role of American Jews in the founding. Neither was thinking particularly clearly about the matter, because neither had truly found its balance after World War II. Both knew the

Levant was important, but neither saw the Levant as a central battleground at that moment. Israel slipped through the cracks.

Once the question of Jewish unity was settled through ruthless action by David Ben Gurion's government, Israel faced a simultaneous threat from all of its immediate neighbors. However, as we have seen, the threat in 1948 was more apparent than real. The northern Levant, Lebanon, was fundamentally disunited — far more interested in regional maritime trade and concerned about control from Damascus. It posed no real threat to Israel. Jordan, settling the eastern bank of the Jordan River, was an outside power that had been transplanted into the region and was more concerned about native Arabs — the Palestinians — than about Israel. The Jordanians secretly collaborated with Israel. Egypt did pose a threat, but its ability to maintain lines of supply across the Sinai was severely limited and its genuine interest in engaging and destroying Israel was more rhetorical than real. As usual, the Egyptians could not afford the level of effort needed to move into the Levant. Syria by itself had a very real interest in Israel's defeat, but by itself was incapable of decisive action.

The exterior lines of Israel's neighbors prevented effective, concerted action. Israel's interior lines permitted efficient deployment and redeployment of force. It was not obvious at the time, but in retrospect we can see that once Israel existed, was united and had even limited military force, its survival was guaranteed. That is, so long as no great power was opposed to its existence.

From its founding until the Camp David Accords re-established the Sinai as a buffer with Egypt, Israel's strategic problem was this: So long as Egypt was in the Sinai, Israel's national security requirements outstripped its military capabilities. It could not simultaneously field an army, maintain its civilian economy and produce all the weapons and supplies needed for war. Israel had to align itself with great powers who saw an opportunity to pursue other interests by arming Israel.

Israel's first patron was the Soviet Union — through Czechoslovakia — which supplied weapons before and after 1948 in the hopes of using Israel to gain a foothold in the eastern Mediterranean. Israel, aware of the risks of losing autonomy, also moved into a relationship with a declining great power that was fighting to retain its empire: France. Struggling to hold onto Algeria and in constant tension with Arabs, France saw Israel as a natural ally. And apart from the operation against Suez in 1956, Israel saw in France a patron that was not in a position to reduce Israeli autonomy. However, with the end of the Algerian war and the realignment of France in the Arab world, Israel became a liability to France and, after 1967, Israel lost French patronage.

Israel did not become a serious ally of the Americans until after 1967. Such an alliance was in the American interest. The United States had, as a strategic imperative, the goal of keeping the Soviet navy out of the Mediterranean or, at least, blocking its unfettered access. That meant that Turkey, controlling the Bosporus, had to be kept in the American bloc. Syria and Iraq shifted policies in the late 1950s and by the mid-1960s had been armed by the Soviets. This made Turkey's position precarious: If the Soviets pressed from the north while Syria and Iraq pressed from the south, the outcome would be uncertain, to say the least, and the global balance of power was at stake.

The United States used Iran to divert Iraq's attention. Israel was equally useful in diverting Syria's attention. So long as Israel threatened Syria from the south, it could not divert its forces to the north. That helped secure Turkey at a relatively low cost in aid and risk. By aligning itself with the interests of a great power, Israel lost some of its room for maneuver: For example, in 1973, it was limited by the United States in what it could do to Egypt. But those limitations aside, it remained autonomous internally and generally free to pursue its strategic interests.

The end of hostilities with Egypt, guaranteed by the Sinai buffer zone, created a new era for Israel. Egypt was restored to its traditional position, Jordan was a marginal power on the east bank, Lebanon was in its normal, unstable mode, and only Syria was a threat. However, it was a threat that Israel could easily deal with. Syria by itself could not threaten the survival of Israel.

Following Camp David (an ironic name), Israel was in its Davidic model, in a somewhat modified sense. Its survival was not at stake. Its problems — the domination of a large, hostile population and managing events in the northern Levant — were subcritical (meaning that, though these were not easy tasks, they did not represent fundamental threats to national survival, so long as Israel retained national unity). When unified, Israel has never been threatened by its neighbors. Geography dictates against it.

Israel's danger will come only if a great power seeks to dominate the Mediterranean Basin or to occupy the region between Afghanistan and the Mediterranean. In the short period since the fall of the Soviet Union, this has been impossible. There has been no great power with the appetite and the will for such an adventure. But 15 years is not even a generation, and Israel must measure its history in centuries.

It is the nature of the international system to seek balance. The primary reality of the world today is the overwhelming power of the United States. The United States makes few demands on Israel that matter. However, it is the nature of things that the United States threatens the interests of other great powers who, individually weak, will try to form coalitions against it. Inevitably, such coalitions will arise. That will be the next point of danger for Israel.

In the event of a global rivalry, the United States might place onerous requirements on Israel. Alternatively, great powers might move into the Jordan River valley or ally with Syria, move into Lebanon or ally with Israel. The historical attraction of the eastern shore of the Mediterranean would focus the attention of such a power and lead to attempts to assert control over the Mediterranean or create a secure Middle Eastern empire. In either event, or some of the others discussed, it would create a circumstance in which Israel might face a Babylonian catastrophe or be forced into some variation of a Persian or Roman subjugation.

Israel's danger is not a Palestinian rising. Palestinian agitation is an irritant that Israel can manage so long as it does not undermine Israeli unity. Whether it is managed by domination or by granting the Palestinians a vassal state matters little. Nor can Israel be threatened by its neighbors. Even a unified attack by Syria and Egypt would fail, for the reasons discussed. Israel's real threat, as can be seen in history, lies in the event of internal division and/or a great power coveting Israel's geographical position, marshalling force that is beyond its capacity to resist. Even that can be managed if Israel has a patron whose interests involve denying the coast to another power.

Israel's reality is this. It is a small country, yet it must manage threats arising far outside of its region. It can survive only if it maneuvers with great powers commanding enormously greater resources. Israel cannot match the resources and, therefore, it must be constantly clever. There are periods when it is relatively safe because of great power alignments, but its normal condition is one of global unease. No nation can be clever forever, and Israel's history shows that some form of subordination is inevitable. Indeed, it is to a very limited extent subordinate to the United States now.

For Israel, the retention of a Davidic independence is difficult. Israel's strategy must be to manage its subordination effectively by dealing with its patron cleverly, as it did with Persia. But cleverness is not a geopolitical concept. It is not permanent, and it is not assured. And that is the perpetual crisis of Jerusalem.

The Geopolitics of the Palestinians
Jan. 15, 2009

Dealing with the geopolitics of a nation without a clearly defined geography is difficult. The geography within which Palestinians currently live is not the area they claim as their own, nor are their current boundaries recognized as legitimate by others. The Palestinians do not have a state that fully controls the territory in which they live, nor can their existing governing entity, the Palestinian National Authority, be regarded as speaking for all Palestinians. A range of things that a state must have in order to be a state, from an economy to a military force, either do not exist or exist in forms that are not fully mature. It is therefore impossible to speak of the geopolitics of "Palestine" as if it were a nation-state. We will begin instead by speaking of the geopolitics of the Palestinians — and in a departure from other installments in this series, we do not begin with geography, but end there.

In raising the notion of a Palestinian geopolitics, we already enter an area of controversy, because there are those — and this includes not only Israelis but Arabs as well — who would argue that there is no such thing as a Palestinian nation, that there is no distinct national identity that can be called Palestinian. But while that might have been true 100 years ago or even 50, it is certainly no longer true. If there was no Palestinian nation in the past, there certainly is one now, and — like many nations — it was born in battle. A nation has more than an identity. It has a place, a location. And that location determines its behavior. To understand Hamas' actions in Gaza, or Israel's for that matter, it is necessary to consider first the origins and then the geopolitics of the Palestinians. This is a story that we have told before, but it is key to understanding the geopolitics of the region.

The Origins of Palestinian Geopolitics

The story begins with the Ottoman Empire, which controlled the Middle East from 1517 to 1918, when World War I ended. The Ottomans divided the Middle East into provinces, one of which was Syria. Under the Ottomans, the Syria province encompassed what is today Syria, Lebanon, Jordan and Israel. Constantinople (Istanbul), the Ottoman seat, sided with the Germans in World War I. As a result, after the war the victorious British and French dismantled the Ottoman Empire, and the province of Syria came under British and French rule. Under a secret wartime French-British deal, known as the Sykes-Picot agreement, the province was divided on a line running from Mount Hermon due west to the sea. The area to the north was placed under French control; the area to the south was placed under British control.

The French region was further subdivided. The French had been allied with the Maronite Christians during a civil war that raged in the region in the 1860s. Paris owed them a debt, so it turned the predominantly Maronite region of Syria into a separate state, naming it Lebanon after the dominant topographical characteristic of the region, Mount Lebanon. As a state, Lebanon had no prior reality, nor even a unified ethno-sectarian identity; its main unifying feature was that, demographically, it was dominated by French allies.

The British region also was divided. The Hashemites, who ruled the western Hejaz region of the Arabian Peninsula, had supported the British, rising up against the Ottomans. In return, the British had promised to make them rulers of Arabia after the war. But in addition to the Hashemites, London was also allied with the French and with other tribes against the Ottomans, and thus could not make the Hashemites the unquestioned rulers of all of Arabia

THE GEOPOLITICS OF ISRAEL AND THE PALESTINIANS

OTTOMAN EMPIRE, 1914

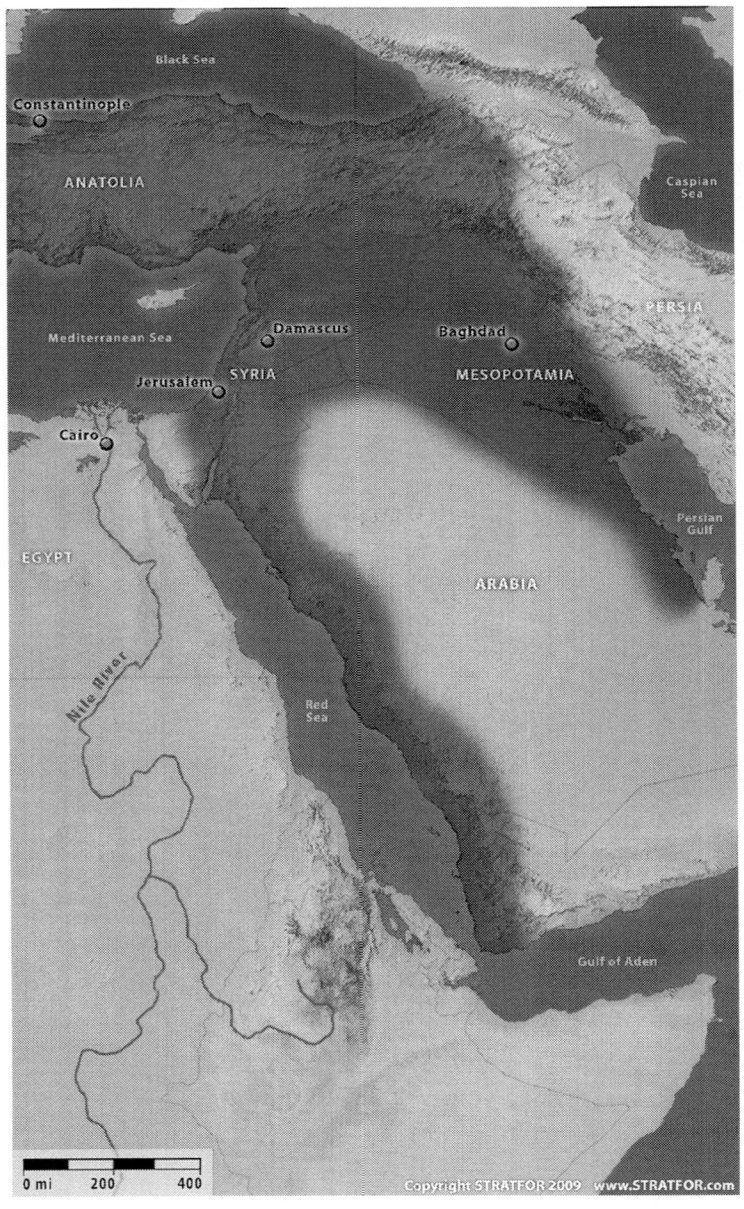

(the Peninsula as well as the Levant). Furthermore, the Sauds in 1900 had launched the reconquest of Arabia from Kuwait, and had gained control over the eastern and central parts of the peninsula. By the mid-1920s, the Hashemites lost control over the peninsula to the Sauds, paving the way for the eventual creation of Saudi Arabia.

But by then the British had moved the Hashemites to an area in the northern part of the peninsula, on the eastern bank of the Jordan River. Centered on the town of Amman, they named this protectorate carved from Syria "Trans-Jordan," as in "the other side of the Jordan River," since it lacked any other obvious identity. After the British withdrew in 1948, Trans-Jordan became contemporary Jordan. The Hashemites also had been given another kingdom, Iraq, in 1921, which they lost to a coup by Nasserist military officers in 1958.

West of the Jordan River and south of Mount Hermon was a region that had been an administrative district of Syria under the Ottomans. It had been called "Philistia" for the most part, undoubtedly after the Philistines whose Goliath had fought David thousands of years before. Names here have history. The term Philistine eventually came to be known as Palestine, a name derived from ancient Greek — and that is what the British named the region, whose capital was Jerusalem.

Significantly, while the people of this area were referred to as Palestinians, a demand for a Palestinian state was virtually nonexistent in 1918. The European concept of national identity at this time was still very new to the Arab region of the Ottoman Empire. There were clear distinctions in the region, however. Arabs were not Turks. Muslims were

THE GEOPOLITICS OF ISRAEL AND THE PALESTINIANS

BRITISH MANDATE, 1920-1948

THE IMPORTANCE OF PLACE

PROPOSED U.N. PARTITION PLAN, 1947 (REJECTED)

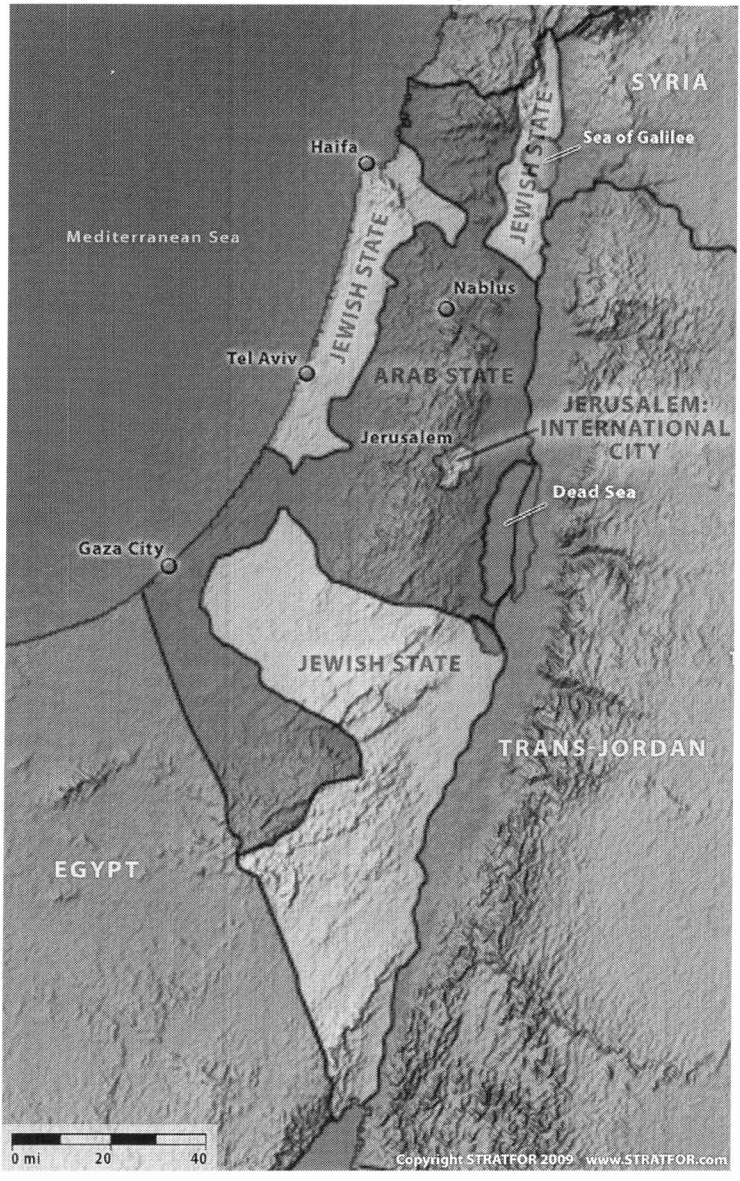

not Christians, nor were they Jews. Within the Arab world there were religious, tribal and regional conflicts. For example, there were tensions between the Hashemites from the Arabian Peninsula and the Arabs settled in Trans-Jordan, but these were not defined as tensions between the country of Jordan and the country of Palestine. They were very old and very real, but they were not thought of in national terms.

European Jews had been moving into this region under Ottoman rule since the 1880s, joining relatively small Jewish communities that had existed there (and in most other Arab regions) for centuries. The movement was part of the Zionist movement, which — motivated by European definitions of nationalism — sought to create a Jewish state in the region. The Jews came in small numbers, settling on land purchased for them by funds raised by Jews in Europe. Usually, this land was bought from absentee landlords in Cairo and elsewhere who had gained ownership of the land under the Ottomans. The landlords sold the land out from under the feet of Arab tenants, dispossessing them. From the Jewish point of view, this was a legitimate acquisition of land. From the tenants' point of view, this was a direct assault on their livelihood and eviction from land their families had farmed for generations. And so it began first as real estate transactions, winding up as partition, dispossession and conflict after World War II and the massive influx of Jews after the Holocaust.

Rather, the key factor was the view that Palestine was a province of the sovereign entity known as Syria, and those we call Palestinians today were simply Syrians. The Syrians have always been uncomfortable with the concept of Palestinian statehood — though not with the destruction of

THE IMPORTANCE OF PLACE

1949 ARMISTICE FOLLOWING THE 1948 ARAB-ISRAELI WAR

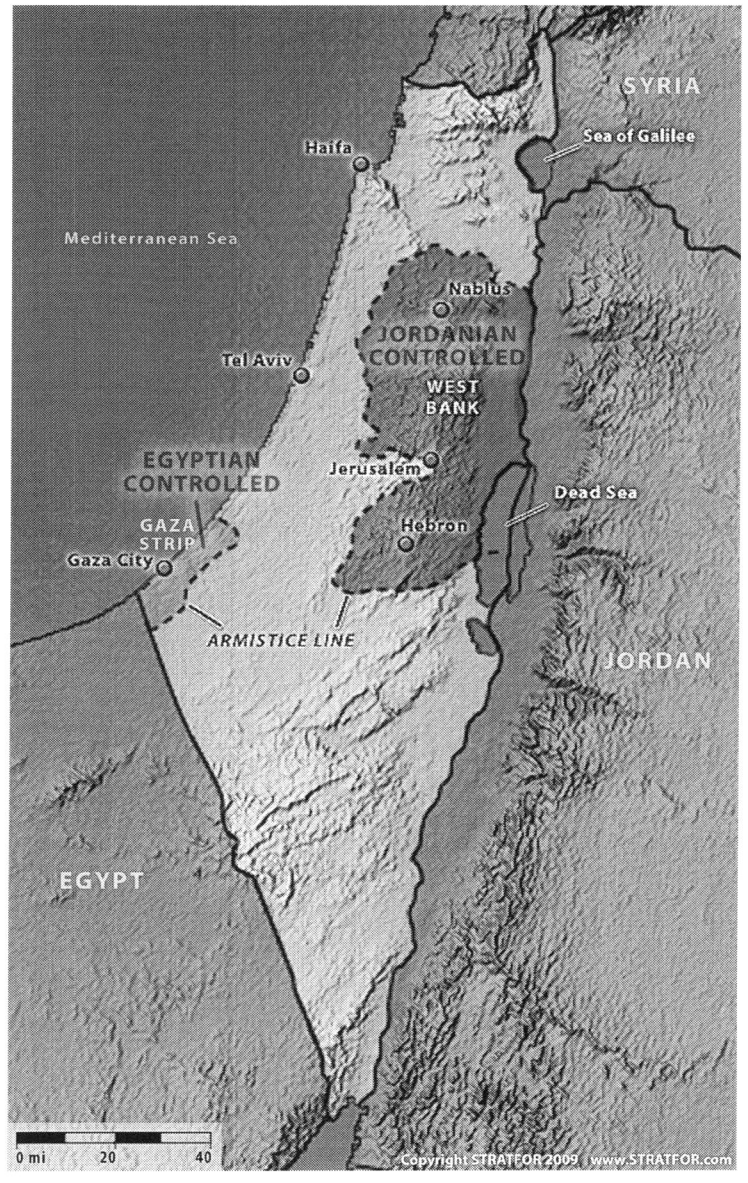

Israel — and actually invaded Lebanon in the 1970s to destroy the Palestine Liberation Organization (PLO) and Fatah.
 The Jordanian view of the Palestinians was even more uncomfortable. The Hashemites were very different from the region's original inhabitants. After the partition of British-administered Palestine in 1948, Jordan took control of the West Bank and East Jerusalem. But there were deep tensions with the Palestinians, and the Hashemites saw Israel as a guarantor of Jordanian security against the Palestinians. They never intended to see an independent Palestinian state (they could have granted it independence between 1948 and 1967), and in September 1970 they fought a bloody war against the Palestinians, forcing the PLO out of Jordan and into Lebanon. The Jordanians remain very fearful that the last vestige of the Hashemite monarchy could collapse under the weight of Palestinians in the kingdom and in the West Bank, paving the way for a Palestinian takeover of Jordan.
 The Egyptians also have been uncomfortable with the Palestinians. Under the monarchy and prior to the rise of Gamal Abdul Nasser in 1952, Egypt was hostile to Israel's creation. But when the Egyptian army drove into what is now called Gaza in 1948, Cairo saw Gaza as an extension of the Sinai Peninsula — as it saw the Negev Desert. It viewed the region as an extension of Egypt, not as a distinct state.
 Nasser's position was even more radical. He had a vision of a single, united Arab republic, both secular and socialist, and thought of Palestine not as an independent state but as part of this United Arab Republic (which actually was founded as a federation of Egypt and Syria from 1958 to 1961). Yasser Arafat was in part a creation of Nasser's

THE IMPORTANCE OF PLACE

ISRAELI TERRITORIAL GAINS FOLLOWING THE SIX-DAY WAR, 1967

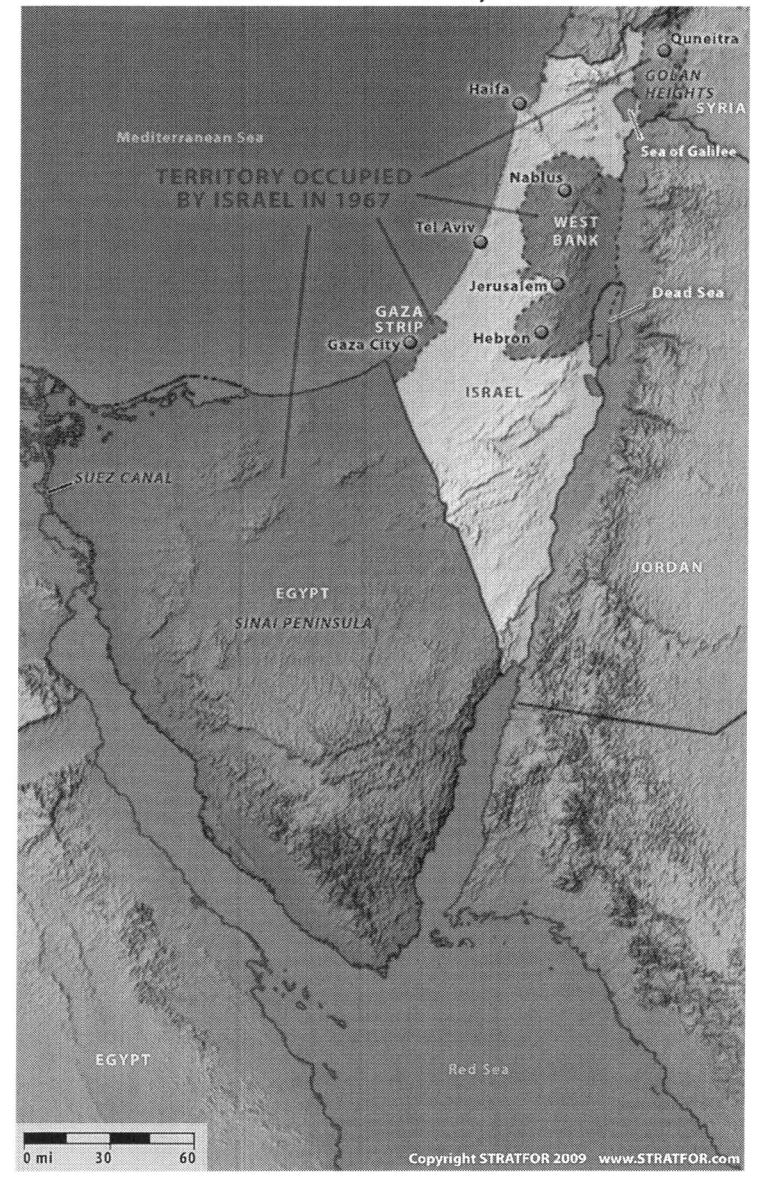

secular socialist championing of Arab nationalism. The liberation of Palestine from Israel was central to Arab nationalism, though this did not necessarily imply an independent Palestinian republic.

Arafat's role in defining the Palestinians in the mind of Arab countries also must be understood. Nasser was hostile to the conservative monarchies of the Arabian Peninsula. He intended to overthrow them, knowing that incorporating them was essential to a united Arab regime. These regimes in return saw Arafat, the PLO and the Palestinian movement generally as a direct threat.

It is critical to understand that Palestinian nationalism did not simply emerge over and against Israel. That is only one dimension. Palestinian nationalism represented a challenge to the Arab world as well: to Syrian nationalism, to Jordanian nationalism, to Nasser's vision of a United Arab Republic, to Saudi Arabia's sense of security. If Arafat was the father of Palestinian nationalism, then his enemies were not only the Israelis but also the Syrians, the Jordanians, the Saudis and — in the end — the Egyptians as well.

The Palestinian Challenge Beyond Israel

Palestinian nationalism's first enemy is Israel, but if Israel ceased to exist, the question of an independent Palestinian state would not be settled. All of the countries bordering such a state would have serious claims on its lands, not to mention a profound distrust of Palestinian intentions. The end of Israel thus would not guarantee a Palestinian state. One of the remarkable things about Israel's Operation Cast Lead in Gaza was that no Arab state moved quickly to take aggressive steps on the Gazans' behalf. Apart from ritual condemnation, weeks into the offensive no Arab state had done anything significant. This was not accidental: The Arab states do not view the creation of a Palestinian state as being in their interests. They do view the destruction of Israel as being in their interests, but since they do not expect that to come about anytime soon, it is in their interest to reach some sort of understanding with the Israelis while keeping the Palestinians contained.

The emergence of a Palestinian state in the context of an Israeli state also is not something the Arab regimes see as in their interest — and this is not a new phenomenon. They have never simply acknowledged Palestinian rights beyond the destruction of Israel. In theory, they have backed the Palestinian cause, but in practice they have ranged from indifferent to hostile toward it. Indeed, the major power that is now attempting to act on behalf of the Palestinians is Iran — a non-Arab state whose involvement is regarded by the Arab regimes as one more reason to distrust the Palestinians.

Therefore, when we say that Palestinian nationalism was born in battle, we do not mean simply that it was born in the conflict with Israel: Palestinian nationalism also was formed in conflict with the Arab world, which has both sustained the Palestinians and abandoned them. Even when the Arab states have gone to war with Israel, as in 1973, they have fought for their own national interests — and for the destruction of Israel — but not for the creation of a Palestinian state. And when the Palestinians were in battle against the Israelis, the Arab regimes' responses ranged from indifferent to hostile.

Geography

The Palestinians are trapped in regional geopolitics. They also are trapped in their own particular geography. First, and most obviously, their territory is divided into two widely separated states: the Gaza Strip and the West Bank. Second, these two places are very different from each other. Gaza is a nightmare into which Palestinians fleeing Israel were forced by the Egyptians. It is a social and economic trap. The West Bank is less unbearable, but regardless of what happens to Jewish settlements, it is trapped between two enemies, Israel and Jordan. Economically, it can exist only in dependency on its more dynamic neighboring economy, which means Israel.

Gaza has the military advantage of being dense and urbanized. It can be defended. But it is an economic catastrophe, and given its demographics, the only way out of its condition is to export workers to Israel. To a lesser extent, the same is true for the West Bank. And the Palestinians have been exporting workers for generations. They have immigrated to countries in the region and around the world. Any peace agreement with Israel would increase the exportation of labor locally, with Palestinian labor moving into the Israeli market. Therefore, the paradox is that while the current situation allows a degree of autonomy amid social, economic and military catastrophe, a settlement would dramatically undermine Palestinian autonomy by creating Palestinian dependence on Israel.

The only solution for the Palestinians to this conundrum is the destruction of Israel. But they lack the ability to destroy Israel. The destruction of Israel represents a far-fetched scenario, but were it to happen, it would necessitate that other nations hostile to Israel — both bordering the Jewish state and elsewhere in the region — play a major role. And if they did play this role, there is nothing in their history, ideology or position that indicates they would find the creation of a Palestinian state in their interests. Each would have very different ideas of what to do in the event of Israel's destruction.

Therefore, the Palestinians are trapped four ways. First, they are trapped by the Israelis. Second, they are trapped by the Arab regimes. Third, they are trapped by geography, which makes any settlement a preface to dependency. Finally, they are trapped in the reality in which they exist, which rotates from the minimally bearable to the unbearable. Their choices are to give up autonomy and nationalism in favor of economic dependency, or retain autonomy and nationalism expressed through the only means they have — wars that they can at best survive, but can never win.

The present division between Gaza and the West Bank had its origins in the British mandate. Palestine was partitioned between Jews and Arabs. In the wake of the 1948 War, Arabs lost control of what was Israel; the borders that emerged from this war and lasted until 1967 are still recognized as Israel's international boundary. The area called the West Bank was part of Jordan. The area called Gaza was effectively under Egyptian control. Numbers of Arabs remained in Israel as Israeli citizens, and played only a marginal role in Palestinian affairs thereafter.

During the 1967 Arab-Israeli war, Israel occupied both Gaza and the West Bank, taking direct military and administrative control of both regions. The political

THE GEOPOLITICS OF ISRAEL AND THE PALESTINIANS

PALESTINIAN TERRITORIES, PRESENT DAY

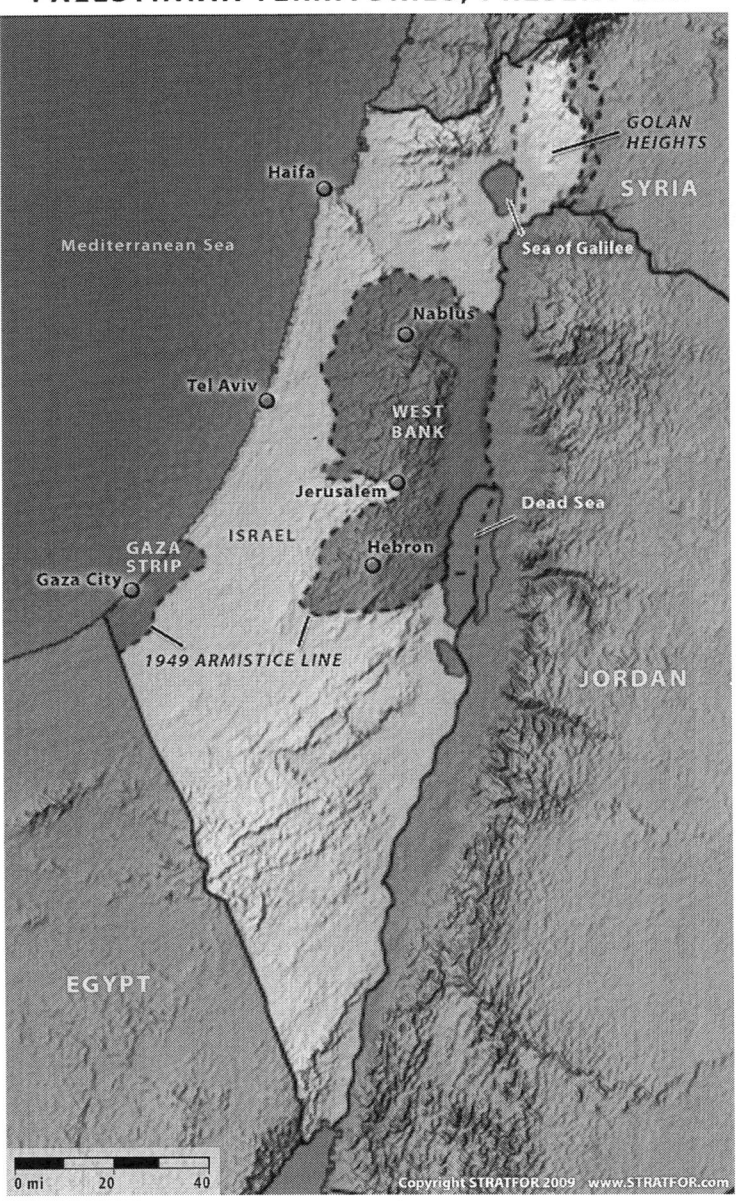

apparatus of the Palestinians, organized around the PLO — an umbrella organization of diverse Palestinian groups — operated outside these areas, first in Jordan, then in Lebanon after 1970, and then in Tunisia after the 1982 invasion of Lebanon by Israel. The PLO and its constituent parts maintained control of groups resisting Israeli occupation in these two areas.

The idea of an independent Palestinian state, since 1967, has been geographically focused on these two areas. The concept has been that, following mutual recognition between Israel and the Palestinians, Palestine would be established as a nation-state based in Gaza and the West Bank. The question of the status of Jerusalem was always a vital symbolic issue for both sides, but it did not fundamentally affect the geopolitical reality.

Gaza and the West Bank are physically separated. Any axis would require that Israel permit land or air transit between them. This is obviously an inherently unstable situation, although not an impossible one. A negative example would be Pakistan during the 1947-1971 period, with its eastern and western wings separated by India. This situation ultimately led to the 1971 separation of these two territories into two states, Pakistan and Bangladesh. On the other hand, Alaska is separate from the rest of the United States, which has not been a hindrance. The difference is obvious. Pakistan and Bangladesh were separated by India, a powerful and hostile state. Alaska and the rest of the United States were separated by Canada, a much weaker and less hostile state. Following this analogy, the situation between Israel and the hypothetical Palestine resembles the Indo-

Pakistani equation far more than it does the U.S.-Canadian equation.

The separation between the two Palestinian regions imposes an inevitable regionalism on the Palestinian state. Gaza and the West Bank are very different places. Gaza is about 25 miles long and no more than 7.5 miles at its greatest width, with a total area of about 146 square miles. According to 2008 figures, more than 1.5 million Palestinians live there, giving it a population density of about 11,060 per square mile, roughly that of a city. Gaza is, in fact, better thought of as a city than a region. And like a city, its primary economic activity should be commerce or manufacturing, but neither is possible given the active hostility of Israel and Egypt. The West Bank, on the other hand, has a population density of a little over 600 people per square mile, many living in discrete urban areas distributed through rural areas.

In other words, the West Bank and Gaza are entirely different universes with completely different dynamics. Gaza is a compact city incapable of supporting itself in its current circumstances and overwhelmingly dependent on outside aid; the West Bank has a much higher degree of self-sufficiency, even in its current situation. Under the best of circumstances, Gaza will be entirely dependent on external economic relations. In the worst of circumstances, it will be entirely dependent on outside aid. The West Bank would be neither. Were Gaza physically part of the West Bank, it would be the latter's largest city, making Palestine a more complex nation-state. As it is, the dynamic of the two regions is entirely different.

Gaza's situation is one of pure dependency amid hostility. It has much less to lose than the West Bank and far less room for maneuver. It also must tend toward a more uniform response to events. Where the West Bank did not uniformly participate in the intifada — towns like Hebron were hotbeds of conflict while Jericho remained relatively peaceful — the sheer compactness of Gaza forces everyone into the same cauldron. And just as Gaza has no room for maneuver, neither do individuals. That leaves little nuance in Gaza compared to the West Bank, and compels a more radical approach than is generated in the West Bank.

If a Palestinian state were created, it is not clear that the dynamics of Gaza, the city-state, and the West Bank, more of a nation-state, would be compatible. Under the best of circumstances, Gaza could not survive at its current size without a rapid economic evolution that would generate revenue from trade, banking and other activities common in successful Mediterranean cities. But these cities have either much smaller populations or much larger areas supported by surrounding territory. It is not clear how Gaza could get from where it is to where it would need to be to attain viability.

Therefore, one of the immediate consequences of independence would be a massive outflow of Gazans to the West Bank. The economic conditions of the West Bank are better, but a massive inflow of hundreds of thousands of Gazans, for whom anything is better than what they had in Gaza, would buckle the West Bank economy. Tensions currently visible between the West Bank under Fatah and Gaza under Hamas would intensify. The West Bank could not absorb the population flow from Gaza, but the Gazans could not remain in Gaza except in virtually total dependence on foreign aid.

The only conceivable solution to the economic issue would be for Palestinians to seek work en masse in more dynamic economies. This would mean either emigration or entering the work force in Egypt, Jordan, Syria or Israel. Egypt has its own serious economic troubles, and Syria and Jordan are both too small to solve this problem — and that is completely apart from the political issues that would arise after such immigration. Therefore, the only economy that could employ surplus Palestinian labor is Israel's.

Security concerns apart, while the Israeli economy might be able to metabolize this labor, it would turn an independent Palestinian state into an Israeli economic dependency. The ability of the Israelis to control labor flows has always been one means for controlling Palestinian behavior. To move even more deeply into this relationship would mean an effective annulment of Palestinian independence. The degree to which Palestine would depend on Israeli labor markets would turn Palestine into an extension of the Israeli economy. And the driver of this will not be the West Bank, which might be able to create a viable economy over time, but Gaza, which cannot.

From this economic analysis flows the logic of Gaza's Hamas. Accepting a Palestinian state along lines even approximating the 1948 partition, regardless of the status of Jerusalem, would not result in an independent Palestinian state in anything but name. Particularly for Gaza, it would solve nothing. Thus, the Palestinian desire to destroy Israel flows not only from ideology and/or religion but from a rational analysis of what independence within the current geographical architecture would mean: a divided nation with profoundly different interests, one part utterly incapable of self-sufficiency, the other part potentially capable of it — but only if it jettisons responsibility for Gaza.

It follows that support for a two-state solution will be found most strongly in the West Bank and not at all in Gaza. But in truth, the two-state solution is not a solution to Palestinian desires for a state, since that state would be independent in name only. At the same time, the destruction of Israel is an impossibility so long as Israel is strong and other Arab states are hostile to Palestinians.

Palestine cannot survive in a two-state solution. It therefore must seek a more radical outcome — the elimination of Israel — that it cannot possibly achieve by itself. The Palestinian state is thus an entity that has not fulfilled any of its geopolitical imperatives and which does not have a direct line to achieve them. What an independent Palestinian state would need in order to survive is:

- The recreation of the state of hostilities that existed prior to Camp David between Egypt and Israel. Until Egypt is strong and hostile to Israel, there is no hope for the Palestinians.

- The overthrow of the Hashemite government of Jordan, and the movement of troops hostile to Israel to the Jordan River line.

- A major global power prepared to underwrite the military capabilities of Egypt and those of whatever eastern power moves into Jordan (Iraq, Iran, Turkey or a coalition of the foregoing).

- A shift in the correlation of forces between Israel and its immediate neighbors, which ultimately would result in the collapse of the Israeli state.

Note that what the Palestinians require is in direct opposition to the interests of Egypt and Jordan — and to those of much of the rest of the Arab world, which would not welcome Iran or Turkey deploying forces in their heartland. It would also require a global shift that would create a global power able to challenge the United States and motivated to arm the new regimes. In any scenario, however, the success of Palestinian statehood remains utterly dependent upon outside events somehow working to the Palestinians' advantage.

The Palestinians have always been a threat to other Arab states because the means for achieving their national aspiration require significant risk-taking by other states. Without that appetite for risk, the Palestinians are stranded. Therefore, Palestinian policy always has been to try to manipulate the policies of other Arab states or, failing that, to undermine and replace those states. This divergence of interest between the Palestinians and existing Arab states always has been the Achilles' heel of Palestinian nationalism. The Palestinians must defeat Israel to have a state, and to achieve that they must have other Arab states willing to undertake the primary burden of defeating Israel. This has not been in the interests of other Arab states, and therefore the Palestinians have persistently worked against them, as we see again in the case of Egypt.

Paradoxically, while the ultimate enemy of Palestine is Israel, the immediate enemy is always other Arab countries. For there to be a Palestine, there must be a sea change not only in the region but also in the global power configuration and in Israel's strategic strength. The Palestinians can neither live with a two-state solution nor achieve the destruction of Israel. Nor do they have room to retreat. They can't go forward and they can't go back. They are trapped, as Palestinians seemingly destined not to have a Palestine.

CHAPTER 2: Groundwork

Good Intentions and the Road to Hell
July 10, 2000

The latest Camp David talks are part of a chain, stretching back to Wye Plantation and Oslo. All were supposed to lay the groundwork for lasting peace. But why will the latest talks succeed where all the others have failed? To begin, what exactly is the president trying to achieve? With his tenure winding to a close, Clinton is looking to his legacy. Camp David, after all, is where President Carter presided over an Israeli-Egyptian settlement. Clinton would clearly like to leave behind the equivalent of Carter's Camp David Accords.

In itself, this is not an ignoble motive. Presidents have a right to be concerned with their place in history, and striking an Israeli-Palestinian settlement is not a bad legacy. The problem that will arise is not one of intention. The problem is whether the goal — a formal settlement — is first attainable and second worth attaining. The attempt to move beyond informal settlements to formal ones may make the situation worse rather than better. In seeking his place in history, Clinton's good intentions may set the stage for a substantial deterioration of the situation.

To understand the profound difference between the first Camp David Accords and these, consider the difference between Israeli-Egyptian relations and Israeli-Palestinian relations. In strict geopolitical terms, Egypt and Israel shared nothing but a border. Indeed, the border itself was artificial; Israel proper and Egypt proper were separated physically by the Sinai wasteland. The Sinai created the opportunity for peace because it allowed the separation of two nations.

But no such buffer is conceivable between Israel and the Palestinians. Even when Israel blockades the West Bank, hundreds of thousands of Palestinians and Israeli citizens are intermingled in Israel proper. In Jerusalem, boundaries are measured not in miles but in streets and buildings. These two peoples are intimately connected by the economy as well. The Palestinians of the West Bank and Gaza occupy territories that are simply not viable without access to other markets for both products and labor. Countless Palestinians have migrated to other countries, true, but those who remain need Israel as a place to work. In turn, Israel depends on the Palestinian labor force for cheap labor.

Economics aside, the fact is that Israelis and Palestinians cannot get out of one another's way. Nor can they easily define their relationship to each other. In a fundamental sense, Israelis and Palestinians both regard the other as usurpers and intruders. Each regards the other as a historical victimizer, and each can make eloquent and persuasive arguments in defense of its own victimization. Instead of being marginal, these sensibilities go to the heart of the political culture of each people. Zionism cannot dispense with the idea that the Jewish exile and return was a moral imperative and so, whoever inhabited the land during their absence was a squatter. Palestinian nationalism is built on the idea that the inhabitants of the land now called Israel were the unique victims of alien settlers who stole the land and dispossessed the people. Each political culture is defined over and against the other. A formal settlement at Camp David would require that one side give the other some formal, explicit acknowledgement of claims to the land.

To do so, each side would have to modify its own understanding of history. Israelis would have to treat Palestinians as other than interlopers, with legitimate rights. Palestinians would have to formally accept that Israelis have real rights, too. To do this formally would require a wrenching redefinition of both Zionism and Palestinian nationalism. The thorn in the heart of this problem is not whether each leadership is prepared to live with such an understanding; both sides live each day with the inescapable reality of the presence of the other.

The question, however, is whether the political systems of either Israel or the Palestinians could endure the formal acknowledgement of the reality. Can either side cross the chasm between tacit understanding and formal agreement? The Israeli political system, for one, is a fragmented constellation of political parties. In election after election, regardless of whether Labor or Likud wins, neither side has enough votes in the Knesset to govern without a coalition. As in any democracy, coalition building in Israel is a mixture of high-minded principle and pork-barrel politics. Who controls the housing budget is intermingled with the relationship between secular and religious authorities.

The question of the Palestinians is thrown into this mélange of interest-group politics and deep, principled division. After all, Palestinians and their rights intersect everything from housing strategy to a Jew's obligation to the Torah's understanding of the land that was promised. The Israeli political system is not only fragile but also brittle.

In this context, minor parties threaten to bring down governments over pork-barrel issues and can hold matters of grand strategy hostage to those issues. Simply raising the Palestinian issue provides minor parties with tremendous leverage over any government. The result is the rapid destabilization of any Israeli government that tries to deal with the matter; most governments are unstable even if the Palestinian matter is never raised. Until there is a revolution in Israeli voting patterns, Israelis simply don't have the political ability to deal with the fundamental issue on the table.

Nor, for that matter, do the Palestinians. The structure of the Palestinian polity is such that it must always generate a faction that stands in opposition to dealing with Israel. Conditions in Gaza are wretched, and conditions in the West Bank are nearly as bad. Any agreement with Israel threatens to lock into place a system of political and economic relationships that are at best barely tolerable. An argument can be made that Israel is an unavoidable reality and that, for better or worse, accommodation has to take place. This was the position of Arafat's elders. Once, he opposed it. Now, this is Arafat's position, criticized as it is by younger opponents. The problem here is the Palestinian version of pork-barrel politics. The misery of the Palestinian people is not equally distributed. Arafat maintains his position within Fatah and within the Palestine National Authority (PNA) by practicing the carrot-and-stick strategy of rewarding friends and coercing enemies. He is therefore perceived — by some — as an Israeli collaborator. But more important, he is seen as an obstacle to their economic interest and political ambition.

As in Israel, fundamental matters of principle intersect with more prosaic political and economic interests. Given the poverty of the Gaza and West Bank, a fairly large segment of the population sees itself as the simultaneous victim of both Israel and Arafat's PNA. Arafat simply doesn't have enough chips with which to build a broad enough coalition to support him. As a result, the promise of peace is only minimally enticing, since it seems to promise long-term economic misery. Many are frightened by a formal peace because they are afraid it will lock them into a double marginalization: first behind the Jews, second behind the PNA. This is compounded by the deep ideological and national principles that block acknowledging the permanence of Israel. The result is a permanent faction prepared to block any formal settlement.

This faction understands fully the deepest Israeli fears, fears carefully fanned by their Israeli counterparts. The Israeli fear is rooted in geography: Any Palestinian entity will become a staging ground for an army rolling across Israel's narrow waist. At the very least, it will be a staging ground for terrorists. Even if the Clinton administration thinks it has the implicit acquiescence of Hamas, another faction will arise to carry out the role of spoiler, giving Israeli hard-liners an excuse to crack down. As the Israelis crack down, the anti-Arafat faction in Hamas and elsewhere can claim that Israel has no intention of allowing Palestinian autonomy. Further, they can argue that Arafat himself is either a dupe or an agent of the Israelis. As the situation grows out of control on the Palestinian side, the brittle Israeli political structure shatters, leading to a political vacuum — a new election that settles nothing.

It is important to understand that Israeli-Palestinian co-habitation has come a long way since the end of the intifada. While the more extreme dreams of Oslo have not come to pass, there is a Palestinian government, however it is called, in increasing control of the West Bank. This is a tremendous event, unimaginable, say, in 1973. But the most important elements have been the implicit ones, not the explicit ones — the formal announcements of talks aimed at a final, breakthrough agreement. In a very practical way, rooted in the Middle East, the formal understandings and the way in which things actually work are not intimately connected. Far more progress has been made in accommodating the fears and needs of both sides by not addressing them formally.

Which brings us back to Camp David. It seems the president, at the very least, has chosen the wrong place. It is not that he won't get a document out of Camp David. Neither the Israelis nor the Palestinians are going to be the ones to sabotage the talks. Each side is too savvy about American power and about the media's perception to simply walk out of the summit. Some piece of paper is likely to emerge. The problem is that whatever emerges will hurt both Barak and Arafat, the very figures to which U.S. policy is tied. Washington actively supported Barak against Netanyahu just as it backs Arafat against Hamas. It is, therefore, extraordinary that the administration is forcing both men into a negotiation that can cause severe, if not fatal, political damage at home. Formal recognition — on paper — will provide opportunities for political destabilization rather than increased security.

Two metaphors are likely to apply. The first — that the road to hell is paved with good intentions — quickly comes to mind. The second — that a straight line is not necessarily the fastest route to peace — will do as well. Peace is not always best achieved by peace talks. Sometimes, not discussing peace is the best course. Clinton's need for a legacy and the reality of Israeli-Palestinian relations are on a collision course. It is likely that both will lose at Camp David.

Sharon's Wall
Aug. 5, 2003

Israel, under Prime Minister Ariel Sharon, is in the process of building a wall that ultimately will separate Israelis and Palestinians along a line roughly — but not at all precisely — identical to the cease-fire lines that held from 1948 until 1967. The wall is far from complete, but the logic for it is self-evident: It represents Israel's attempt to impose a reality that will both satisfy the Jewish state's fundamental security needs and the minimal political demands of the Palestinians without requiring Palestinian agreement or acquiescence.

It is an extraordinary attempt at applied geopolitics. The question is whether it will work. Let's begin with the technical aspect. It is possible, with substantial effort, to create a barrier that not only stops large-scale population movements but seriously inhibits small-scale movements as well. The Iron Curtain was more than a rhetorical term: We once walked along the Austro-Hungarian border, seeing watch towers with machine guns and search lights; concertina wire; dense mine fields; and wide, clear-cut killing fields where infiltrators or exfiltrators could be observed during the day or at night in the glare of search lights and flares.

The line ran from the Baltic to the Yugoslav border. It did work — there was certainly some movement across, but only at great risk and probable failure. The purpose of the Iron Curtain was to prevent eastern Europeans from moving to the west and away from Soviet occupation. It was difficult to build and maintain, but it was built and it did work quite well. It was built with World War II technology. The Israeli project will involve more modern sensor technology, both human and machine. Movement will not be spotted by the luck of the flare but with sound sensors, ground radar and unmanned aerial vehicles. The point is that from a technical standpoint, if the Iron Curtain could work, this can work.

The challenge is political and military, not technical. From the Israeli standpoint, the driving force is desperation. Suicide attacks have achieved what Palestinian planners hoped for — convincing the Israelis the status quo cannot be maintained. The bombings have convinced Israeli leaders that the continued physical occupation of the West Bank and the Gaza Strip are not an option. The problem the Israelis have had to confront is that simply retreating and abandoning the occupation might not solve their strategic problem. From the Israeli standpoint, the problem of the Oslo accords is that they rested on a political decision by the Palestinians, who had to guarantee that they would abandon further claims — and military operations — against the state of Israel in return for Israeli withdrawal.

The last two years convinced Israeli leaders of two things: first, that any guarantee from a Palestinian government was unstable and could not be regarded as permanent; and second, that even if the Palestinian government was able to maintain its own commitment to an agreement, it was incapable of guaranteeing that all Palestinian factions would honor it. Israel observed the ability of the Irish Republican Army, ETA and other groups to continue operations without or against state sanctions. Since the absolute minimum concession from the Palestinians had to be the cessation of suicide bombings and related actions against Israel, this posed an insuperable problem. On the one hand, the status quo was untenable; on the other, a political foundation for withdrawal appeared to be unattainable. Israel was trapped between two impossible realities.

For Israel, the Camp David Accords with Egypt provided the basic model for negotiations with Arabs. Camp David consisted of three parts:

- Egyptian recognition that Israel could not be destroyed through military action.

- Israeli recognition that Egypt was capable — as in 1973 — of carrying out military operations that were too costly for Israel.

- Recognition that the Sinai Desert could serve not only as Israel's strategic depth in maneuver warfare but equally well as a demilitarized buffer zone large enough to prevent surprise attack.

It was on this basis that Menachem Begin, Sharon's intellectual and strategic mentor, reached agreement with Egypt to end hostilities — an agreement that remains the strategic foundation of Israel's national security policy today. The crucial piece was that the deal did not rely on Egypt's good will. The buffer was sufficiently large that any Egyptian violation would be quickly noticed and could be responded to militarily. In other words, Israel could keep control of its fate without holding Egyptian territory. The Oslo agreement was an attempt to apply this same principle to the Palestinian question. It was built on the Palestinian recognition that Palestinians could not destroy Israel militarily and the Israeli recognition that the cost of occupation was greater than Israel could rationally bear.

What was missing — and always has been — was a third step. There has been no possibility of disengagement. From the Israeli viewpoint, this has meant that any settlement depended on both the continued goodwill of the Palestinian state and the absence of dissident anti-Israeli movements. Since neither could be guaranteed, no solution was possible. Hence, the fence. It should be noted that the creation of a fixed barrier violates all Israeli military thinking. The state's military doctrine is built around the concept of mobile warfare. Israel's concern is with having sufficient strategic depth to engage an enemy attack and destroy it, rather than depending on a fixed barrier. From a purely military standpoint, Israel would view this barrier as an accident waiting to happen. The view of barriers (such as the Suez Canal) is that they can all be breached using appropriate, massed military force. This is the critical point. From the Israeli standpoint, the wall is not a military solution. It is not a Maginot Line designed to protect against enemy main force; it is designed to achieve a very particular, very limited and very important paramilitary goal. It is designed to stop the infiltration of Palestinian paramilitaries into Israel without requiring either the direct occupation of Palestinian territory — something that has not worked anyway — or precluding the creation of a Palestinian state.

It is not a Maginot Line, it is an Iron Curtain. And this is where the conceptual problems start to crop up. The Iron Curtain was a fairly impermeable barrier. Nothing moved across it except at very clearly defined and limited checkpoints. The traffic at these checkpoints was quite low during most of the Cold War, and there was ample opportunity for inspection and interrogation of traffic headed in either direction. Even so, these checkpoints were used by Western intelligence both to penetrate Warsaw Pact countries and to extract people. There were other points along the frontier where more informal traffic crossed, but what never took place — particularly after the Berlin Wall went up — was mass, interzonal traffic on a continual basis. The Iron Curtain never looked like the U.S.-Mexican border, nor can the U.S.-Mexican border become an Iron Curtain because neither the United States nor Mexico wants that to happen. Trade is continual, and the movement of illegal labor from Mexico to the United States is informally viewed by the U.S. government as necessary.

The U.S.-Mexican border is therefore a barrier to almost nothing — virtually everything, legal and illegal, flows across the barrier. As much as it is disliked, the flow is needed. For the Israeli security model to work, economic relations between Israel and Palestine will have to be ruptured. The idea of the controlled movement of large numbers of workers, trucks and so on across the border is incompatible with the idea of the fence as a security barrier. Once movement is permitted, movement is permitted. Along with that movement will come guerrillas, weapons and whatever anyone wants to send across. You cannot be a little bit pregnant on this: Either Israel seals its frontier, or the fence is a waste of steel and manpower. If the wall is not continual and impermeable, it may as well not be there.

The geopolitical idea underlying the fence is that that it will not be permeable. If this goal is achieved, regardless of where the final line of the fence will be, then economic and social relations between Israel and Palestine will cease to exist except through third-party transit. Forgetting the question of Jerusalem — for if Jerusalem is an open city, the fence may as well not be built — this poses a huge strategic challenge. Palestinians historically have depended on Israel economically. If Israel closes off its frontiers, the only contiguous economic relationship will be with Jordan. In effect, Palestine would become a Jordanian dependency. However, it will not be clear over time which is the dog and which is the tail. Jordan already has a large Palestinian population that has, in the past, threatened the survival of the Hashemite Bedouin regime. By sealing off Palestinian and

Israeli territories, the Israelis would slam Palestine and Jordan together. Over the not-so-long term, this could mean the end of Hashemite Jordan and the creation of a single Palestinian state on both sides of the Jordan River.

There are Israelis — including Sharon, in our view — who would not object to this outcome. They have argued that the Hashemite presence in Amman has long distorted the reality in the region. The Hashemite regime was installed by Britain after World War I. In the opinion of some Israelis, Jordan ought to be the real Palestine. Therefore, if the fence results in the fall of the Jordanian monarchy and the creation of a unitary Palestinian state, these Israelis would find this a positive development. Indeed, one argument goes that a Jordan with boundaries roughly analogous to pre-1967 lines would undermine Palestinian radical movements by creating a more stable, less aggressive Palestinian nation-state.

Two other scenarios exist. In one, the Hashemites survive and drive many of the Palestinians on the east bank of the Jordan into the West Bank, the Israelis maintain their cordon sanitaire and the Palestinian nation-state becomes an untenable disaster — trapped between two enemies, Israel and Jordan. Israel would not object to this, but the problem is that the level of desperation achieved in Palestine might prove so chaotic that it either would threaten Israeli national security or set into motion processes in the Arab world — and among Israel's Western allies — that would increase pressure on Israel. In other words, the Israelis would wind up strategically where they started, with the non-trivial exception of fewer or no suicide bombings.

The other scenario is that the Palestinians do merge with Jordan, but — given the dynamics of the Arab and

Islamic worlds — the new nation-state does not moderate but instead generates, with assistance from other Arabs, a major military strike force for whom the fence represents at most a minor tactical barrier. Under this scenario, the consequences would be a return to the strategic situation of 1948-1967 (except for Egypt's participation), with a potentially more powerful enemy to the east. If Egypt were to change its policies, the outcome could be strategically disastrous for Israel.

The problem with the fence, therefore, is this:

- If it is to be effective as a barrier, it must be nearly absolute; large-scale movement cannot be permitted.

- If a Palestinian state is isolated, it will develop a dependency on Jordan that could topple the Hashemite regime, creating a potential strategic threat to Israel.

The fence strategy works only if the Palestinian-Jordanian relationship yields a politically moderate Palestinian state. That might happen, but there is no reason to be certain that it will. The essential purpose of the fence is to give Israel control of its security. The problem is that Israel can control the construction of the fence, but not the evolution of events after the fence is built. At some point in the process, Israel becomes dependent on the actions of others.

This is Israel's core strategic dilemma. At some point, no matter what it does, it becomes dependent on events that are not under its control. In some scenarios, solving the problem of suicide bombings leads to a massive deterioration of Israel's strategic position. Israeli leaders obviously want to avoid that, but the fence pushes out the strategic problem and paradoxically intensifies it instead of solving it. Israeli security continues to depend on the decisions of the Palestinians. The fence is an attempt to take control of Israel's future out of Palestinian hands and place it securely in Israeli hands, but the fact is that what the Palestinians do will continue to affect Israel's security. As is frequently the case in this world, Israel does not have good choices. It has to make some bad ones work.

CHAPTER 3: Turning Points

The Death of Arafat
Nov. 12, 2004

That Yasser Arafat's death marks the end of an era is so obvious that it hardly bears saying. The nature of the era that is ending and the nature of the era that is coming, on the other hand, do bear discussing. That speaks not only to the Arab-Israeli conflict but also to the evolution of the Arab world in general.

In order to understand Arafat's life, it is essential to understand the concept "Arab," and to understand its tension with the concept "Muslim," at least as Arafat lived it out. In general, ethnic Arabs populate North Africa and the area between the Mediterranean and Iran, and between Yemen and Turkey. This is the Arab world. It is a world that is generally — but far from exclusively — Muslim, although the Muslim world stretches far beyond the Arab world.

To understand Arafat's life, it is much more important to understand the Arab impulse than to understand the Muslim impulse. Arafat belonged to that generation of Arab who visualized the emergence of a single Arab nation, encapsulating all of the religious groups in the Arab world, and one that was essentially secular in nature. This vision did not originate with Arafat but with his primary patron, Gamal Abdul Nasser, the founder of modern Egypt and of the idea of a United Arab Republic. No sense can be made of Arafat's life without first understanding Nasser's.

Nasser was born into an Egypt that was ruled by a weak and corrupt monarchy and effectively dominated by Britain. He became an officer in the Egyptian army and fought competently against the Israelis in the 1948 war. He emerged from that war committed to two principles: The first was recovering Egyptian independence fully; the second was making Egypt a modern, industrial state. Taking his bearing from Kamal Ataturk, who founded the modern Turkish state, Nasser saw the military as the most modern institution in Egypt, and therefore the instrument to achieve both independence and modernization. This was the foundation of the Egyptian revolution.

Nasser was a practicing Muslim of sorts — he attended mosque — but he did not see himself as leading an Islamic revolution at all. For example, he placed numerous Coptic Christians in important government positions. For Nasser, the overriding principle was not Islam but Arabism. Nasser dreamed of uniting the Arabs in a single entity, whose capital would be Cairo. He believed that until there was a United Arab Republic, the Arabs would remain the victims of foreign imperialism.

Nasser saw his prime antagonists as the traditional monarchies of the Arab world. Throughout his rule, Nasser tried to foment revolutions, led by the military, that would topple these monarchies. Nasserite or near-Nasserite revolutions toppled Iraqi, Syrian and Libyan monarchies. Throughout his rule, he tried to bring down the Jordanian,

Saudi and other Persian Gulf regimes. This was the constant conflict that overlaid the Arab world from the 1950s until the death of Nasser and the rise of Anwar Sadat.

Geopolitics aligned Nasser's ambitions with the Soviet Union. Nasser was a socialist but never a Marxist. Nevertheless, as he confronted the United States and threatened American allies among the conservative monarchies, he grew both vulnerable to the United States and badly in need of a geopolitical patron. The Soviets were also interested in limiting American power and saw Nasser as a natural ally, particularly because of his confrontation with the monarchies.

Nasser's view of Israel was that it represented the intrusion of British imperialism into the Arab world, and that the conservative monarchies, particularly Jordan, were complicit in its creation. For Nasser, the destruction of Israel had several uses. First, it was a unifying point for Arab nationalism. Second, it provided a tool with which to prod and confront the monarchies that tended to shy away from confrontation. Third, it allowed for the further modernization of the Egyptian military — and therefore of Egypt — by enticing a flow of technology from the Soviet Union to Egypt. Nasser both opposed the existence of Israel and saw its existence as a useful tool in his general project.

It is important to understand that for Nasser, Israel was not a Palestinian problem but an Arab problem. In his view, the particular Arab nationalisms were the problem, not the solution. Adding another Arab nationalism — Palestinian — to the mix was not in his interest. The Zionist injustice was against the Arab nation and not against the Palestinians as a particular nation. Nasser was not alone in this view. The

Syrians saw Palestine as a district of Syria, stolen by the British and French. They saw the Zionists as oppressors, but against the Syrian nation. The Jordanians, who held the West Bank, saw the West Bank as part of the Jordanian nation and, by extension, the rest of Palestine as a district of Jordan. Until the 1967 war, the Arab world was publicly and formally united in opposing the existence of Israel, but much less united on what would replace Israel after it was destroyed. The least likely candidate was an independent Palestinian state.

Prior to 1967, Nasser sponsored the creation of the Palestine Liberation Organization (PLO) under the leadership of Ahmed al Shukairi. It was an entirely ineffective organization that created a unit that fought under Egyptian command. Since 1967 was a disaster for Nasser, "fought" is a very loose term. The PLO was kept under tight control, careful avoiding the question of nationhood and focusing on the destruction of Israel.

After the 1967 war, the young leader of the PLO's Fatah faction took control of the organization. Yasser Arafat was a creature of Nasser, politically and intellectually. He was an Arabist. He was a modernizer. He was a secularist. He was aligned with the Soviets. He was anti-American. Arafat faced two disparate questions in 1967. First, it was clear that the Arabs would not defeat Israel in a war, probably in his lifetime; what, therefore, was to be done to destroy Israel? Second, if the only goal was to destroy the Israelis, and if that was not to happen anytime soon, then what was to become of the Palestinians? Arafat posed the question more radically: Granted that Palestinians were part of the Arab revolution, did they have a separate identity of their own, as did Egyptians or Libyans? Were they simply Syrians or Jordanians? Who were they?

Asserting Palestinian nationalism was not easy in 1967, because of the Arabs themselves. The Syrians did not easily recognize their independence and sponsored their own Palestinian group, loyal to Syria. The Jordanians could not recognize the Palestinians as separate, as their own claim to power even east of the Jordan would be questionable, let alone their claims to the West Bank. The Egyptians were uneasy with the rise of another Arab nationalism.

Simultaneously, the growth of a radical and homeless Palestinian movement terrified the monarchies. Arafat knew that no war would defeat the Israelis. His view was that a two-tiered approach was best. On one level, the PLO would make the claim on behalf of the Palestinian people, for the right to statehood on the world stage. On the other hand, the Palestinians would use small-scale paramilitary operations against soft targets — terrorism — to increase the cost throughout the world of ignoring the Palestinians.

The Soviets were delighted with this strategy, and their national intelligence services moved to facilitate it by providing training and logistics. A terror campaign against Israel's supporters would be a terror campaign against Europe and the United States. The Soviets were delighted by anything that caused pain and destabilized the West. The cost to the Soviets of underwriting Palestinian operations, either directly or through various Eastern European or Arab intelligence services, was negligible. Arafat became a revolutionary aligned with the Soviets.

There were two operational principles. The first was that Arafat himself should appear as the political wing of the movement, able to serve as an untainted spokesman for Palestinian rights. The second was that the groups that carried out the covert operations should remain complex and murky. Plausible deniability combined with unpredictability was the key.

Arafat created an independent covert capability that allowed him to make a radical assertion: that there was an independent Palestinian people as distinct as any other Arab nation. Terrorist operations gave Arafat the leverage to assert that Palestine should take its place in the Arab world in its own right.

If Palestine was a separate nation, then what was Jordan? The Hashemite kingdom consisted of Bedouins driven out of Arabia. The majority of the population was not Bedouin but had its roots in the west — hence, they were Palestinians. If there was a Palestinian nation, then why were they being ruled by Bedouins from Arabia? In September 1970, Arafat made his move. Combining a series of hijackings of Western airliners with a Palestinian rising in Jordan, Arafat attempted to seize control of Jordan. He failed, and thousands of Palestinians were slaughtered by Hashemite and Pakistani mercenaries. (Coincidentally, the military unit dispatched to Jordan was led by then-Brigadier Zia-ul-Haq, who later ruled Pakistan from 1977 to 1988 as a military dictator.)

Arafat's logic was impeccable. His military capability was less than perfect.

Arafat created a new group — Black September — that was assigned the task of waging a covert war against the Israelis and the West. The greatest action, the massacre of Israeli athletes at the Munich Olympics in 1972, defined the next generation. Israel launched a counter-operation to destroy Black September, and the pattern of terrorism and counter-terrorism swirling around the globe was set. The PLO was embedded in a network of terrorist groups sponsored by the Soviets that ranged from Japan to Italy. The Israelis became part of a multinational counter-attack. Neither side could score a definitive victory.

But Arafat won the major victory. Nations are frequently born of battle, and the battles that began in 1970 and raged until the mid-1990s established an indelible principle — there is now, if there was not before, a nation called Palestine. This was critical, because as Nasser died and his heritage was discarded by Anwar Sadat, the principle of the Arab nation was lost. It was only through the autonomous concept of Palestinian nationalism that Arafat and the PLO could survive.

And this was Arafat's fatal crisis. He had established the principle of Palestine, but what he had failed to define was what that Palestinian nation meant and what it wanted. The latter was the critical point. Arafat's strategy was to appear the statesman restraining uncontrollable radicals. He understood that he needed Western support to get a state, and he used this role superbly. He appeared moderate and malleable in English, radical and intractable in Arabic. This was his insoluble dilemma.

Arafat led a nation that had no common understanding of its goal. There were those who wanted to recover a part of Palestine and be content. There were those who wanted to recover part of Palestine and use it as a base of operations to retake the rest. There were those who would accept no intermediate deal but wanted to destroy Israel.

Arafat's fatal problem was that, in the course of creating the Palestinian nation, he had convinced all three factions that he stood with them.

Like many politicians, Arafat had made too many deals. He had successfully persuaded the West that he genuinely wanted a compromise and that he could restrain terrorism. But he had also persuaded Palestinians that any deal was merely temporary, and others that he wouldn't accept any deal. By the time of the Oslo accords, Arafat was so tied up in knots that he could not longer speak for the nation he created. More precisely, the Palestinians were so divided that no one could negotiate on their behalf, confident in his authority. Arafat kept his position by sacrificing his power.

By the 1990s, the space left by the demise of pan-Arabism had been taken by the rise of Islamist religiosity. Hamas, representing the view that there is a Palestinian nation but that it should be understood as part of the Islamic world under Islamic law, had become the most vibrant part of the Palestinian polity. Nothing was more alien from Arafat's thinking than Hamas. It ran counter to everything he had learned from Nasser.

However — and this is Arafat's tragedy — by the time Hamas emerged as a power, he had lost the ability to believe in anything but the concept of the Palestinians and his place as its leader. As Hamas rose, Arafat became entirely tactical. His goal was to retain position if not power, and toward that end, he would do what was needed. A lifetime of tactics had destroyed all strategy.

His death in Paris was a farce of family and courtiers. It fitted the end he had created, because his last years were lived in a round of clever maneuvers leading nowhere. The Palestinians are left now without strategy, only tactics. There is no one who can speak for the Palestinians and be listened to as authoritative. Arafat created the Palestinian nation and utterly disrupted the Palestinian state. He left a clear concept on the one hand, chaos on the other.

It is interesting to wonder what would have happened if Arafat had won in Jordan in 1970, while Nasser was still alive. But that wasn't going to happen, because Arafat's fatal weakness was visible even then. The concept was clear — but instead of meticulously planning a rising, Arafat improvised, playing politics within the PLO when he should have been managing combat operations. The chaos and failure that marked Black September became emblematic of his life.

Arafat succeeded in one thing, and perhaps that is enough — he created the Palestinian nation against all enemies, Arab and non-Arab. The rest was the endless failure of pure improvisation.

The Gaza Withdrawal and Israel's Permanent Dilemma
Aug. 17, 2005

Israel has begun its withdrawal from Gaza. As with all other territorial withdrawals by Israel, such as that from the Sinai or from Lebanon, the decision is controversial within the Jewish state. It represents the second withdrawal from land occupied in the 1967 war, and the second from land that houses significant numbers of anti-Israeli fighters. Since these fighters will not be placated by the Israeli withdrawal — given that there is no obvious agreement of land for an enforceable peace — the decision by the Israelis to withdraw from Gaza would appear odd. In order to understand what is driving Israeli policy, it is necessary to consider Israeli geopolitical reality in some detail.

Israel's founders, taken together, had four motives for founding the state:

- To protect the Jews from a hostile world by creating a Jewish homeland.

- To create a socialist (not communist) Jewish state.

- To resurrect the Jewish nation in order to re-assert Jewish identity in history.

- To create a nation based on Jewish religiosity and law rather than Jewish nationality alone.

The idea of safety, socialism, identity and religiosity overlapped to some extent and were mutually exclusive in other ways. But each of these tendencies became a fault line in Israeli life. Did Israel exist simply so that Jews would be safe — was Israel simply another nation among many? Was Israel to be a socialist nation, as the Labor Party once envisioned? Was it to be a vehicle for resurrecting Jewish identity, as the Revisionists wanted? Was it to be a land governed by the Rabbinate? It could not be all of these things. Thus, these were ultimately contradictory visions tied together by a single certainty: None of these visions were possible without a Jewish state. All arguments in Israel devolve to these principles, but all share a common reality — the need for the physical protection of Israel.

In order for there to be a Jewish state, it must be governed by Jews. If it is also to be a democratic state, as was envisioned by all but a few of the fourth (religiosity) strand of logic, then it must be a state that is demographically Jewish.

This poses the first geopolitical dilemma for Israel: Whatever the historical, moral or religious arguments, the fact was that at the beginning of the 20th century, the land identified as the Jewish homeland — Palestine — was inhabited overwhelmingly by Arabs. A Jewish and democratic state could be achieved only by a demographic transformation. Either more Jews would have to come to Palestine, or Arabs would have to leave, or a combination of the two would have to occur. The Holocaust caused Jews who otherwise would have stayed in Europe to come to Palestine. The subsequent creation of the state of Israel caused Arabs to leave, and Jews living in Arab countries to come to Israel.

However, this demographic shift was incomplete, leaving Israel with two strategic problems. First, a large number of Arabs, albeit a minority, continued to live in Israel. Second, the Arab states surrounding Israel — which perceived the state as an alien entity thrust into their midst — viewed themselves as being in a state of war with Israel.

Ultimately, Israel's problem was that dealing with the external threat inevitably compounded the internal threat.

Israel's Strategic Disadvantage

Israel was at a tremendous strategic disadvantage. First, it was vastly outnumbered in the simplest sense: There were many more Arabs who regarded themselves as being in a state of war with Israel than there were Jews in Israel. Second, Israel had extremely long borders that were difficult to protect. Third, the Israelis lacked strategic depth. If all of their neighbors — Egypt, Jordan, Syria and Lebanon — were joined by the forces of more distant Arab and Islamic states, Israel would find it difficult to resist. And if all of these forces attacked simultaneously in a coordinated strike, Israel would find it impossible to resist.

Even if the Arabs did not carry out a brilliant stroke, cutting Israel in half on a Jerusalem-Tel Aviv line (a distance of perhaps 20 miles), Israel would still lose an extended war with the Arabs. If the Arabs could force a war of attrition on Israel, in which they could impose an attrition rate of perhaps 1 percent per day of forces on the forward edge of the battle area, Israel would not be able to hold for more than a few months at best. In the 20th century, an attrition rate of that level, in a battle space the size of Israel, would be modest. Israel's effective forces rarely numbered more than 250,000 men — the other 250,000 were older reserves with inferior equipment. Extended attritional warfare was not an option for Israel.

Thus, in order for Israel to survive, three conditions were necessary:

- The Arabs must never unite into a single, effective force.

- Israel must choose the time, place and sequence of any war.

- Israel must never face both a war and an internal uprising of Arabs simultaneously.

Israel's strategy was to use diplomacy to prevent the three main adversaries — Egypt, Jordan and Syria — from simultaneously choosing to launch a war. From its founding, Israel always maintained a policy of splitting the front-line states. This was not particularly difficult, given the deep animosities among the Arabs. For example, Israel always maintained a special relationship with Jordan, which had unsatisfactory relations with its own neighbors. Early on, Israel worked to serve as the guarantor of the Jordanian regime's survival. Later, after the Camp David Accords split Egypt off from the Arab coalition, Israel had neutralized two out of three of its potential adversaries. The dynamics of Arab geopolitics and the skill of Israeli diplomacy achieved an outcome that is rarely appreciated. From its founding, Israel managed to prevent simultaneous warfare with its neighbors except at a time and place of its own choosing. It had to maintain a military force capable of taking the initiative in order to have a diplomatic strategy.

But throughout most of its history, Israel had a fundamental challenge in achieving this pre-eminence.

Israel's Geopolitical Problem

The state's military pre-eminence had to be measured against the possibility of diplomatic failure. Israel had to assume that all front-line states would become hostile to it, and that it would have to launch a pre-emptive strike against them all. If this were the case, Israel had this dilemma: Its national industrial base was insufficient to provide it with the technological wherewithal to maintain its military superiority. It was not simply a question of money — all the money in the world could not change the demographics — but also that Israel lacked the manpower to produce all of the weapons it needed and to field an army. Therefore, Israel could survive only if it had a patron that possessed such an industrial base. Israel had to make itself useful to another country.

Israel's first patron was the Soviet Union, through its European satellites. Its second patron was France, which saw Israel as an ally during a time when Paris was trying to hold onto its interests in an increasingly hostile Arab world. Its third patron — but not until 1967 — was the United States, which saw Israel as a counterweight to pro-Soviet Egypt and Syria, as well as a useful base of operations in the eastern Mediterranean.

In 1967, Israel — fearing a coordinated strike by the Arabs and also seeking to rationalize its defensive lines and create strategic depth — launched an air and land attack against its neighbors. Rather than risk a coordinated attack, Israel launched a sequential attack — first against Egypt, then Jordan, then Syria.

The success of the 1967 war gave rise to Israel's current geopolitical crisis. Following the war, Israel had to balance three interests:

- It now occupied the West Bank and Gaza Strip, which contained large, hostile populations of Arabs. A full, peripheral war combined with an uprising in these regions would cut Israeli lines of supply and communication and risk Israel's defeat.

- Israel was now dependent on the United States for its industrial base. But American interests and Israeli interests were not identical. The United States had interests in the Arab world, and had no interest in Israel crushing Palestinian opposition or expelling Palestinians from Israel. Retaining the industrial base and ruthlessly dealing with the Palestinians became incompatible needs.

- Israel had to continue manipulating the balance of power among Arab states in order to prevent a full peripheral war. That, in turn, meant that it was further constrained in dealing with the Palestinian question by force.

Israeli geopolitics created the worst condition of all: Given the second and third considerations, Israel could not crush the Palestinians; but given its need for strategic depth and coherent borders, it could not abandon the occupied territories. It therefore had to continually constrain the Palestinians without any possibility of final victory. It had to be ruthless, which would enflame the Palestinians, but it could never be ruthless enough to effectively suppress them.

The Impermanence of Diplomacy

Israel has managed to maintain the diplomatic game it began in 1948: The Arabs remain deeply split. It has managed to retain its relationship with the United States, even with the end of the Cold War. Given the decline of the conventional threat, Israel's dependency on the United States has actually dwindled. For the moment, the situation is contained.

However — and this is the key problem for Israel — the diplomatic solution is inherently impermanent. It requires constant manipulation, and the possibility of failure is built in. For example, an Islamist rising in Egypt could rapidly generate shifts that Israel could not contain. Moreover, political changes in the United States could end American patronage, without the certainty of another patron emerging. These things are not likely to occur, but they are not inconceivable. Given enough time, anything is possible.

Israel's advantage is diplomatic and cultural. Its ability to split the Arabs, its diplomatic force, is coupled with its technological superiority, a cultural force. But both of these can change. The Arabs might unite, and they might accelerate their technological and military sophistication. Israel's superiority can change, but its inferiority is fixed: Geography and demography put it in an unchangeably vulnerable position relative to the Arabs.

The potential threats to Israel are:

- A united and effective anti-Israeli coalition among the Arabs.

- The loss of its technological superiority and, therefore, the loss of military initiative.

- The need to fight a full peripheral war while dealing with an intifada within its borders.

- The loss of the United States as patron and the failure to find an alternative.

- A sudden, unexpected nuclear strike on its populated heartland.

Therefore, it follows that Israel has three options:

- The first is to hope for the best. This has been Israel's position since 1967.

- The second is to move from conventional deterrence to nuclear deterrence. Israel already possesses this capability, but the value of nuclear weapons is in their deterrent capability, not in their employment. You can't deal with an intifada or with close-in conventional war with nuclear weapons — not given the short distances involved in Israel.

- The third option is to reduce the possibility of disaster as far as possible by increasing the tensions in the Arab world, reducing the incentive for cultural change among the Arabs, eliminating the threat of intifada in time of war, and reducing the probability that the United States will find it in its interests to break with Israel.

Hence, the withdrawal from Gaza. As a base for terrorism, Gaza poses a security threat to Israel. But the true threat from Gaza, and even more the West Bank, lies in the fact that they create a dynamic that decreases Israel's diplomatic effectiveness, risks creating Arab unity, increases the impetus for military modernization and places stress on Israel's relationship with the United States. The terrorist threat is painful. The alternative risks long-term catastrophe.

Some of the original reasons for Israel's founding, such as the desire for a socialist state, are now irrelevant to Israeli politics. And revisionism, like socialism, is a movement of the past. Modern Israel is divided into three camps:

- Those who believe that the survival of Israel depends on disengaging from a process that enrages without crushing the Palestinians, even if it opens the door to terrorism.

- Those who regard the threat of terrorism as real and immediate, and regard the longer-term strategic threats as theoretical and abstract.

- Those who have a religious commitment to holding all territories.

The second and third factions are in alliance but, at the moment, it is the first faction that appears to be the majority. It is not surprising that Prime Minister Ariel Sharon is leading this faction. As a military man, Sharon has a clear understanding of Israel's vulnerabilities. It is clearly his judgment that the long-term threat to Israel comes from the collapse of its strategic position, rather than from terrorism. He has clearly decided to accept the reality of terrorist attacks, within limits, in order to pursue a broader strategic initiative.

Israel has managed to balance the occupation of a hostile population with splitting Arab nation-states since 1967. Sharon's judgment is that, given the current dynamics of the Muslim world, pursuing the same strategy for another generation would be both too costly and too risky. The position of his critics is that the immediate risks of disengagement increase the immediate danger to Israel without solving the long-term problem. If Sharon is right, then there is room for maneuver. But if his critics, including Benjamin Netanyahu, are right, Israel is locked down to an insoluble problem.

That is the real debate.

The New Power in the PNA
Feb. 1, 2006

Hamas has beaten Fatah in a key election and is now the dominant political party among the Palestinians. Many observers expressed surprise at the outcome, but the only thing that should have surprised anyone is that there was surprise. Hamas was facing a corrupt Fatah faction that had been driven into the ground by Yasser Arafat. Arafat's successor, Mahmoud Abbas — who was widely celebrated by Western leaders — is in fact an obscure party functionary whose primary claim to leadership was his relationship with Arafat. While Arafat, the icon of Palestinian nationalism, could not be repudiated, repudiating Abbas was easy. Like the political wing of Fatah, he stood for nothing but the perpetuation of Fatah and the system of patronage that Arafat created. When it came to Abbas, Western media and leaders confused political exhaustion with virtue.

But it was not simply internal Palestinian politics that drove the Hamas victory. A wave of Islamist politics is sweeping the Muslim and Arab worlds, and the Palestinians are far from immune. The Islamist movement is doing far more than simply challenging the West: It is challenging the secular Arabists who were the heirs of the Nasserite tradition. The Islamists are confronting figures like Hosni Mubarak in Egypt. In many ways, Fatah was the embodiment of secular Arabism — the purest form of Nasserism. The Palestinians were among the most secular in the Arab world. Therefore, challenging and defeating Fatah represents a critical moment in the history of the Arab and Muslim world. It represents a new high-water mark for Islamists.

There was yet another process at work in the election. Arafat and the Palestinian National Authority (PNA) that he essentially created and dominated have existed in a complex relationship with Israel. In many ways, the PNA was a creation of Israel, living within boundaries that Israel defined. Whatever its level of involvement in the suicide bombing campaign against Israel, via Marwan Bargouthi and the al-Aqsa Martyrs Brigade, Fatah still accepted the existence of the state of Israel. As a secular movement, it had no inherent moral objection to Israel's existence — only a political objection, and political objections are inherently flexible.

Hamas has a moral objection to Israel's existence, deriving from its understanding of Islamic texts. But it also had serious political objections to Fatah's approach to Israel. From Hamas' point of view, once Arafat had negotiated the existence of a quasi-state — the PNA — he became casual about negotiating the two critical things: first, the definition and rights of the Palestinian nation and, second, the transformation of the sort-of-state the PNA represented into an authentic state. An authentic state, by Hamas' lights, meant a state with an army that it was free to deploy in a clearly defined territory.

Even if Hamas accepted the existence of Israel in some sense, its view was that the other side of the equation had not been fulfilled. Only the illusion — not the reality — of a Palestinian nation-state had been created. Hamas' objection to Fatah was that it had accepted an illusion. Its objection to Abbas was that he was content to preside over an illusion. Corruption, the decline of Arab secularism and the inability of Fatah to articulate the interests of the Palestinians led it to defeat after decades of dominating and defining the Palestinian cause.

The issue today is what Hamas will do with its power. It must be understood that Hamas has not yet reached an unassailable position among the Palestinians: It defeated but did not blow out Fatah. Fatah is still there and can, particularly after a defeat like this, recover. Moreover, Hamas has never faced the problem of governing. Its unity is the unity of an opposition party, and its purity is the purity of a movement that has never had to award contracts for paving roads. There is a vast difference between opposing the rascals in power and taking power yourself. A party unused to ruling can very quickly become everything that it has opposed — a bureaucratized, patronage-driven entity more interested in holding onto power than in governing.

It is very possible that this will happen to Hamas. Certainly, this is what Israelis hope will happen. There is a strand of thinking among Israelis that argues that Hamas' victory is the best hope there is for peace in the Middle East. The logic runs thus: Negotiating with the PNA under Arafat or Abbas was an exercise in futility. Arafat was duplicitous and Abbas powerless. No settlement reached by Fatah would ever have any meaning because Fatah could not deliver the rejectionists among the Palestinians. Hamas embodies the rejectionists. If Hamas were to enter into an agreement — even if it had opposition on its flanks, like Ariel Sharon did on the Israeli side — it ultimately would be able to deliver. And since peace is always made with enemies, better to deal with your worst enemy than with hapless moderates like Abbas.

Moreover, this line accepts that Hamas rejects the right of Israel to exist, that it has waged and can continue to wage suicide bomb attacks in Israel, and that it intends to govern by whipping up religious sentiment that must, by definition, be anti-Israeli. Nevertheless, this reasoning goes, the experience of government will affect Hamas in two ways. First, Hamas has come into power on a tidal wave of hope — but those hopes inevitably will be dashed. Hamas will, in a fairly short period of time, come under criticism for failing to deliver on those hopes. And second, as we have said, because Hamas is ill-prepared for the mechanics of governing, it will commit a series of amateurish errors, further dulling its bright credentials. Therefore, Hamas — a radical Islamist movement with a rejectionist policy — simultaneously will embody the most radical position among Palestinians while transforming into a normal political party. Not only will it be able to negotiate from a position of authority, but its appetite for confrontation will be dulled.

This is a view shared by many Western observers as well as Israelis, but there is, as one can see, a deep contradiction in the thinking. On the one side, Hamas is valued as a powerful revolutionary force — therefore, it can negotiate authoritatively. On the other, it will be moved to negotiate because the experience of governing will exhaust it sufficiently that it will move from radical to routine politics.

Before this question of what Hamas will do with its power can be answered, two immediate challenges are posed to both Israel and the West. Western countries funnel a great deal of aid to the Palestinians. One of the charges made against Arafat was that he, in effect, stole a great deal of that money. It was one of the charges leveled by his Palestinian critics, and one of the ways they wound up in Palestinian jails. At this point, depending on how the PNA reconstitutes itself, that money is likely to be passed to the control of Hamas functionaries. In effect, Hamas will be the recipient of Western aid.

Israel has a similar problem. The Israelis collect a good portion of Palestinian taxes and pass them back to the PNA — one of the reasons we call the PNA a pseudo-state. When the Israelis remit the funds to Palestinian accounts, those accounts will be controlled by Hamas. Hamas has announced its intention to take its own militias and designate them as a Palestinian army. The Israelis have accepted the concept of a Palestinian police and security force, but accepting the existence of a Palestinian army — let alone a Palestinian army that is in reality Hamas' militias — and passing tax funds to them to spend as they wish would challenge the Israeli understanding of what a Palestinian state will mean. Sharon certainly didn't envision that — and with his incapacitation, he has come to embody the gold standard of the Israeli position on the Palestinians.

But forget the Israelis for a moment. Consider the position of the Americans and Europeans. First, all sides have agreed that there should be a Palestinian state and have provided funding to the PNA. Second, all sides believe deeply in the concepts of national self-determination and free elections. Third, all sides oppose terrorism and the kind of suicide bombing campaigns carried out by Hamas. Even those governments most sympathetic to the Palestinians have opposed Hamas' rejection of Israel's right to exist and the suicide campaigns.

So then, we have an ongoing flow of money to a PNA that is seen as the legitimate representative of the Palestinian people, and what appears to be a free and honest election of a group that is regarded by virtually everyone outside the Muslim world as among the least savory of terrorists. A decision must be made fairly quickly. Does the world honor the principle of national self-determination, even when the nation determines it wishes to be governed by people who are regarded as morally reprehensible?

Those who argue for national self-determination and free elections always seem to think that the outcome will be the election of nice folks who'd be at home in Wisconsin. This is as true of the Bush administration as of Amnesty International. It is the universal self-delusion of the West. OK, so now the Palestinian people have spoken, and they have spoken for Hamas. Since Amnesty International has no power, it will be able to finesse its position more easily than the Bush administration — which does have to make a decision.

The decision to be made is clear and must come soon: Does the United States continue to provide funds to the PNA, even if those funds wind up in Hamas' coffers? This question has broad ramifications. One of the goals the United States has set for itself in the war against jihadists is to create an environment in which free elections can be held in the Muslim world. We guess the assumption has been that, given a choice, Muslims would vote for pro-Western, secular regimes. The Palestinians have voted for an anti-Western, religious regime. Which gives — the doctrine of the absolute right to self-determination, or the absolute opposition to groups designated as terrorists?

The Bush administration does not have the luxury of ignoring this one. Unless action is taken, the money will continue to flow. Sending money to Hamas will surely cause the administration to say, "Does not compute, does not compute." Cutting off the money will signal to the Islamic world that the United States is absolutely committed to democratic institutions, unless it doesn't like the outcome.

The Israelis, for their part, will have to figure out whether they want to rupture relations with the PNA by cutting off tax funds collected from the Palestinians. Doing that could result in the resumption of the intifada and suicide bombings. The Israelis have no appetite for this. Thus, the United States and Israel will be regarding each other with fairly blank looks on their faces, wondering, "What do we do now?"

Meanwhile, Hamas will be moving rapidly to take control of the mechanisms of the PNA. They have made a lot of bold promises, and they need to turn their election into a psychological victory. At the moment, their minds are not on international relations but on consolidating their political and psychological position among the Palestinians. To the extent they are looking beyond their immediate realm, they are looking at the Islamic world.

That means that they will be saying and doing things that increase the fervor of their followers and give opponents a sense of their relentless inevitability. Personnel shifts, particularly the replacement of officials known to be close to the West or Israel, will take place quickly. Statements will be made that will be frightening to the West and exhilarating to the Palestinians. In the United States, Israel and Europe, the blank look will turn to serious concern, and the pressure to act will grow.

That will be the critical point. Hamas benefits from a sense of embattlement — the sense that it is confronting the enemies of Islam. As it backs the Israelis and Americans into a corner, and both start reacting, Hamas will increase its strength and authority. It will also look to countries like Saudi Arabia — a fellow Sunni entity, rather than Shiite Iran — and the other Gulf states for support. Some European countries will continue funding Hamas under the theory that engagement will moderate the movement. And that will be the tipping point.

We have never believed that a long-term solution to the Israeli-Palestinian crisis can be found. It is certainly true that if Hamas, in becoming a governing party, is forced by its circumstances to negotiate a settlement with Israel, then our theory will be wrong. But the other possibility is that Hamas, due to internal political considerations as well as the reaction of Israel and the United States, will become more inflexible. We tend to believe that is the likely outcome. But even if it turns out to be the first case, we long have argued that the geographic realities of the Israelis and Palestinians preclude the existence of two viable states. Hamas, even if it enters the peace process, knows the problem and will demand more than Israel can possibly concede.

The peace process is not in worse shape than it was before the Hamas win, because the situation was never any good. The new constellation is interesting, but not all that different. There will be hints of improvement followed by disappointment, coupled with spasms of violence. We don't see how this can change.

CHAPTER 4: Breaking Points

What Went Wrong
Aug. 8, 2006

On May 23, we published a Geopolitical Intelligence Report titled "Break Point." In that article, we wrote: "It is now nearly Memorial Day. The violence in Iraq will surge, but by July 4 there either will be clear signs that the Sunnis are controlling the insurgency — or there won't. If they are controlling the insurgency, the United States will begin withdrawing troops in earnest. If they are not controlling the insurgency, the United States will begin withdrawing troops in earnest. Regardless of whether the [political settlement] holds, the U.S. war in Iraq is going to end: U.S. troops either will not be needed, or will not be useful. Thus, we are at a break point — at least for the Americans."

In our view, the fundamental question was whether the Sunnis would buy into the political process in Iraq. We expected a sign, and we got it in June, when Abu Musab al-Zarqawi was killed — in our view, through intelligence provided by the Sunni leadership. The same night al-Zarqawi was killed, the Iraqis announced the completion of the Cabinet. As part of a deal that finalized the three security positions (defense, interior and national security), the defense ministry went to a Sunni. The United States followed that move by announcing a drawdown of U.S. forces from Iraq, starting with two brigades. All that was needed was a similar signal of buy-in from the Shia — meaning they would place controls on the Shiite militias that were attacking Sunnis. The break point seemed very much to favor a political resolution in Iraq.

It never happened. The Shia, instead of reciprocating the Sunni and American gestures, went into a deep internal crisis. Shiite groups in Basra battled over oil fields. They fought in Baghdad. We expected that the mainstream militias under the Supreme Council for Islamic Revolution in Iraq (SCIRI) would gain control of the dissidents and then turn to political deal-making. Instead, the internal Shiite struggle resolved itself in a way we did not expect: Rather than reciprocating with a meaningful political gesture, the Shia intensified their attacks on the Sunnis. The Sunnis, clearly expecting this phase to end, held back — and then cut loose with their own retaliations. The result was, rather than a political settlement, civil war. The break point had broken away from a resolution.

Part of the explanation is undoubtedly to be found in Iraq itself. The prospect of a centralized government, even if dominated by the majority Shia, does not seem to have been as attractive to Iraqi Shia as absolute regional control, which would guarantee them all of the revenues from the southern oil fields, rather than just most. That is why SCIRI leader Abdel Aziz al-Hakim has been pushing for the creation of a federal zone in the south, similar to that established for the Kurdistan region in the north. The growing closeness between the United States and some Sunnis undoubtedly left the Shia feeling uneasy. The Sunnis may have made a down payment by delivering up al-Zarqawi, but it was far from clear that they would be in a position to make further payments. The Shia reciprocated partially by offering an amnesty for militants, but they also linked the dissolution of sectarian militias to the future role of Baathists in the government, which they seek to prevent. Clearly, there were factions within the Shiite community that were pulling in different directions.

But there was also another factor that appears to have been more decisive: Iran. It is apparent that Iran made a decision not only to not support a political settlement in Iraq but also *to* support Hezbollah in its war with Israel. In a larger sense, Iran decided to simultaneously confront the United States and its ally Israel on multiple fronts — and to use that as a means of challenging Sunnis and, particularly, Sunni Arab states.

The Iranian Logic

This is actually a significant shift in Iran's national strategy. Iran had been relatively cooperative with the United States between 2001 and 2004 — supporting the United States in Afghanistan in a variety of ways and encouraging Washington to depose Saddam Hussein. This relationship was not without tensions during those years, but it was far from confrontational. Similarly, Iran had always had tensions with the Sunni world, but until last year or so, as we can see in Iraq, these tensions had not been venomous.

Two key things have to be borne in mind to begin to understand this shift. First, until the emergence of al Qaeda, the Islamic Republic of Iran had seen itself — and had been seen by others — as being the vanguard of the Islamist renaissance. It was Iran that had confronted the United States, and it was Iran's creation, Hezbollah, that had pioneered suicide bombings, hostage-takings and the like in Lebanon and around the world. But on Sept. 11, 2001, al Qaeda — a Sunni group — had surged ahead of Iran as the embodiment of radical Islam. Indeed, it had left Iran in the role of appearing to be a collaborator with the United States. Iran had no use for al Qaeda but did not want to surrender its position to the Sunni entity.

The second factor that must be considered is Iran's goal in Iraq. The Iranians, who hated Hussein as a result of the eight-year war and dearly wanted him destroyed, had supported the U.S. invasion of Iraq. And they had helped the United States with intelligence prior to the war. Indeed, it could be argued that Iran had provided exactly the intelligence that would provoke the U.S. attack in a way most advantageous to Iran — by indicating that the occupation of Iraq would not be as difficult as might be imagined, particularly if the United States destroyed the Baath Party and all of its institutions. U.S. leaders were hearing what they wanted to hear anyway, but Iran made certain they heard this much more clearly.

Iran had a simple goal: to dominate a post-war Iraq. Iran's Shiite allies in Iraq comprised the majority, the Shia had not resisted the American invasion and the Iranians had provided appropriate support. Therefore, they expected that they would inherit Iraq — at least in the sense that it would fall into Tehran's sphere of influence. For their part, the Americans thought they could impose a regime in Iraq regardless of Iran's wishes, and they had no desire to create an Iranian surrogate in Baghdad. Therefore, though they may have encouraged Iranian beliefs, the goal of the Americans was to create a coalition government that would include all factions. The Shia could be the dominant group, but they would not hold absolute power — and, indeed, the United States manipulated Iraqi Shia to split them further.

We had believed that the Iranians would, in the end, accept a neutral Iraq with a coalition government that guaranteed Iran's interests. There is a chance that this might be true in the end, but the Iranians clearly decided to force a final confrontation with the United States. Tehran used its influence among some Iraqi groups to reject the Sunni overture symbolized in al-Zarqawi's death and to press forward with attacks against the Sunni community. It goes beyond this, inasmuch as Iran also has been forging closer ties with some Sunni groups, who are responding to Iranian money and a sense of the inevitability of Iran's ascent in the region.

Iran could have had two thoughts on its mind in pressing the sectarian offensive. The first was that the United States, lacking forces to contain a civil war, would be forced to withdraw, or at least to reduce its presence in populated areas, if a civil war broke out. This would leave the majority Shia in a position to impose their own government — and, in fact, place pro-Iranian Shia, who had led the battle, in a dominant position among the Shiite community.

The second thought could have been that, even if U.S. forces did not withdraw, Iran would be better off with a partitioned Iraq — in which the various regions were at war with each other, or at least focused on each other, and incapable of posing a strategic threat to Iran. Moreover, if partition meant that Iran dominated the southern part of Iraq, then the strategic route to the western littoral of the Persian Gulf would be wide open, with no Arab army in a position to resist the Iranians. Their dream of dominating the Persian Gulf would still be in reach, while the security of their western border would be guaranteed. So, if U.S. forces did not withdraw from Iraq, Iran would still be able not only to impose a penalty on the Americans but also to pursue its own strategic interests.

This line of thinking also extends to pressures that Iran now is exerting against Saudi Arabia, which has again become a key ally of the United States. For example, a member of the Iranian Majlis recently called for Muslim states to enact political and economic sanctions against Saudi Arabia, which has condemned Hezbollah's actions in the war against Israel. In the larger scheme, it was apparent to the Iranians that they could not achieve their goals in Iraq without directly challenging Saudi interests — and that meant mounting a general challenge to Sunnis. A partial challenge would make no sense: It would create hostility and conflict without a conclusive outcome. Thus, the Iranians decided to broaden their challenge.

The Significance of Hezbollah

Hezbollah is a Shiite movement that was created by Iran out of its own needs for a Tehran-controlled, anti-Israel force. Hezbollah was extremely active through the 1980s and had exercised economic and political power in Lebanon in the 1990s, as a representative of Shiite interests. In this,

Hezbollah had collaborated with Syria — a predominantly Sunni country run by a minority Shiite sect, the Alawites — as well as Iran. Iran and Syria are enormously different countries, with many different interests. Syria's interest was the domination and economic exploitation of Lebanon. But when the United States forced the Syrians out of Lebanon — following the assassination of former Prime Minister Rafik al-Hariri in February 2005 — any interest Syria had in restraining Hezbollah disappeared. Meanwhile, as Iran shifted its strategy, its interest in reactivating Hezbollah — which had been somewhat dormant in relation to Israel — increased.

Hezbollah's interest in being reactivated in this way was less clear. Hezbollah's leaders had aged well: Violent and radical in the 1980s, they had become Lebanese businessmen by the 1990s. They became part of the establishment. But they still were who they were, and the younger generation of Hezbollah members was even more radical. Hezbollah militants had been operating in southern Lebanon for years and, however relatively restrained they might have been, they clearly had prepared for conventional war against the Israelis.

With the current conflict, Hezbollah now has achieved an important milestone: It has fought better and longer than any other Arab army against Israel. The Egyptians and Syrians launched brilliant attacks in 1973, but their forces were shattered before the war ended. Hezbollah has fought and clearly has not been shattered. Whether it wins or loses in the end, Hezbollah will have achieved a massive improvement of its standing in the Muslim world by slugging it out with Israel in a conventional war. If, at the end of this war, Hezbollah remains intact as a fighting force — regardless of the outcome of the campaign in southern Lebanon — its prestige will be enormous.

Within the region, this outcome would shift focus away from the Sunni Hamas or secular Fatah to the Shiite Hezbollah. If this happens simultaneously with the United States losing complete control of the situation in Iraq, the entire balance of power in the region would be perceived to have shifted away from the U.S.-Israeli coalition (appearance is different from reality, but it is still far from trivial) — and the leadership of the Islamist renaissance would have shifted away from the Sunnis to the Shia, at least in the Middle East.

Outcomes

It is not clear that the Iranians expected all of this to have gone quite as well as it has. In the early days of the war, when the Saudis and other Arabs were condemning Hezbollah and it appeared that Israel was going to launch one of its classic lightning campaigns in Lebanon, Tehran seemed to back away — calling for a cease-fire and indicating it was prepared to negotiate on issues like uranium enrichment. Then international criticism shifted to Israel, and Israeli forces seemed bogged down. Iran's rhetoric shifted. Now the Saudis are back to condemning Hezbollah, and the Iranians appear more confident than ever. From their point of view, they have achieved substantial psychological success based on real military achievements. They have the United States on the defensive in Iraq, and the Israelis are having to fight hard to make any headway in Lebanon.

The Israelis have few options. They can continue to fight until they break Hezbollah — a process that will be long and costly but can be achieved. But then they risk Hezbollah shifting to guerrilla war unless their forces immediately withdraw from Lebanon. Alternatively, they can negotiate a cease-fire that inevitably would leave at least part of Hezbollah's forces intact, its prestige and power in Lebanon enhanced and Iran elevated as a power within the region and the Muslim world. Because the Israelis are not going anywhere, they have to choose from a limited menu.

The United States, on the other hand, is facing a situation in Iraq that has broken decisively against it. However hopeful the situation might have been the night al-Zarqawi died, the decision by Iran's allies in Iraq to pursue civil war rather than a coalition government has put the United States into a militarily untenable position. It does not have sufficient forces to prevent a civil war. It can undertake the defense of the Sunnis, but only at the cost of further polarization with the Shia. The United States' military options are severely limited, and therefore, withdrawal becomes even more difficult. The only possibility is a negotiated settlement — and at this point, Iran doesn't need to negotiate. Unless Grand Ayatollah Ali al-Sistani, the top Shiite cleric in Iraq, firmly demands a truce, the sectarian fighting will continue — and at the moment, it is not even clear that al-Sistani could get a truce if he wanted one.

While the United States was focused on the chimera of an Iranian nuclear bomb — a possibility that, assuming everything we have heard is true, remains years away from becoming reality — Iran has moved to redefine the region. At the very least, civil war in Lebanon (where Christians and

Sunnis might resist Hezbollah) could match civil war in Iraq, with the Israelis and Americans trapped in undesirable roles.

The break point has come and gone. The United States now must make an enormously difficult decision. If it simply withdraws forces from Iraq, it leaves the Arabian Peninsula open to Iran and loses all psychological advantage it gained with the invasion of Iraq. If American forces stay in Iraq, it will be as a purely symbolic gesture, without any hope for imposing a solution. If this were 2004, the United States might have the stomach for a massive infusion of forces — an attempt to force a favorable resolution. But this is 2006, and the moment for that has passed. The United States now has no good choices; its best bet was blown up by Iran. Going to war with Iran is not an option. In Lebanon, we have just seen the value of air campaigns pursued in isolation, and the United States does not have a force capable of occupying and pacifying Iran.

As sometimes happens, obvious conclusions must be drawn.

A Glimmer of Hope at Annapolis
Nov. 26, 2007

U.S. President George W. Bush will host a meeting Nov. 27 between Palestinian President Mahmoud Abbas and Israeli Prime Minister Ehud Olmert in Annapolis, Md. This is fairly banal news, as the gathering seems intended to give the impression that the United States cares what happens between the Israelis and the Palestinians. The last such meeting, the Camp David summit between Yasser Arafat and Ehud Barak, sponsored by then-President Bill Clinton, was followed by massive violence. Therefore, the most we have learned to hope for from such meetings is nothing. This one will either be meaningless or catastrophic.

There is an interesting twist to this meeting, however. The Arab League voted to encourage Arab foreign ministers to attend. The Saudis have announced they will be present, along with the Egyptians and Jordanians who were expected there. Even the Syrians said they will attend, as long as the future of the Golan Heights is on the table. We would expect the Israelis to agree to that demand because, with more bilateral issues on the table, less time will need to be devoted to Palestinian issues. And that might suit many of the Arab states that are ambivalent, to say the least, about the Palestinians.

We have written of the complex relations between the Palestinians and the Arabs, although the current situation is even more complex. Abbas is from the Palestinian group Fatah, Arafat's political vehicle. Fatah was historically a secular, socialist group with close ties to Gamal Abdel Nasser's Egypt and the Soviet Union. It also was regarded as a threat to the survival of the Arab monarchies of the Arabian Peninsula. When Syria invaded Lebanon in 1975, it was not to fight the Israelis or the Lebanese Christians but to drive out Fatah. Given this history, it is ironic that the Arab League has decided to sanction attendance at the Annapolis conference. The Saudis and the Syrians are particularly hostile to Fatah, while the Jordanians and the Egyptians have their own problems with the group.

Behind this strange move are the complexities of Palestinian politics. As Palestinian National Authority (PNA) president, Abbas is charged with upholding its charter and executing PNA foreign policy. But another group, Hamas, won the last parliamentary elections and therefore controlled the selection of the prime minister. Such splits are not uncommon in political systems in which there is a strong president and a parliamentary system, as in France.

But in this case the split ripped the Palestinians apart. The problem was not simply institutional but also geographic. The Palestinian territories are divided into two very different parts — the West Bank and the Gaza Strip. The former was dominated by Jordan between 1948 and 1967, the latter by Egypt. They have very different social and economic outlooks and political perspectives. In June, Hamas rose up and took control of Gaza, while Abbas and Fatah retained control of the PNA and the West Bank.

This created an historic transformation. Palestinian nationalism in the context of Israel can be divided into three eras. In the first era, 1948-1967, Palestinian nationalism was a subset of Arab nationalism. Palestine was claimed in whole or in part by Egypt, Jordan and Syria. In the second era, 1967 to mid-2007, Palestinian nationalism came into its own, with an identity and territorial demands distinct from other Arab powers. An umbrella organization, the Palestine Liberation Organization (PLO), consisting of diverse and frequently divided Palestinian movements, presided over the Palestinian national cause, and eventually evolved into the PNA.

Recently, however, a dramatic shift has taken place. This was not simply the Hamas victory in the January 2006 elections, although the emergence of an Islamist movement among the Palestinians represented a substantial shift among a people who were historically secularist. It was not even the fact that by 2007 Hamas stood in general opposition to the tradition of the PLO, meaning not only Fatah but other Palestinian secular groups. The redefinition of the Palestinian issue into one between Islamists and secularists had been going on for a while.

Rather, it was the rising in Gaza that dramatically redefined the Palestinians by creating two Palestinian entities, geographically distinct and profoundly different in outlook and needs. The idea of a Palestinian state in the West Bank and Gaza, divided by Israel, was reminiscent of Pakistan in its first quarter-century of existence — when what is today Pakistan and Bangladesh, divided by India's thousands of miles, were treated as one country. It was a reach.

Suddenly in June, a new reality emerged. Whatever the Palestinian charter said, whatever the U.N. resolutions said, whatever anyone said, there were now two Palestinian entities — "states" is a good word for them, though it upsets everyone, including the Palestinians. Hamas controlled Gaza and Fatah controlled the West Bank, although neither saw this situation as final. The PNA constantly threatened to reassert itself in Gaza, while Hamas threatened to extend its revolution to the West Bank. Either might happen, but for now, the Palestinians have split along geopolitical lines.

From Israel's point of view, this situation poses both a problem and an opportunity. The problem is that Hamas, more charismatic than the tired Fatah, opposes any settlement with Israel that accepts the Jewish state's existence. The opportunity is, of course, that the Palestinians are now split and that Hamas controls the much poorer and weaker area of Gaza. If Hamas can be kept from taking control of the West Bank, and if Fatah is unable to reassert its control in Gaza, the Israelis face an enemy that not only is weakened but also engaged in a long-term civil war that will weaken it further.

To bring this about, it is clear what Israel's goal should be at Annapolis. That is, to do everything it can to strengthen the position of Abbas, Fatah and the PNA. It is ironic, of course, that Israel should now view Fatah as an asset that needs to be strengthened, but history is filled with such ironies. Israel's goal at Annapolis is to cede as much as possible to Abbas, both territorially and economically, to intensify the split in the Palestinian community and try to strengthen the hand of the secularists. Israel, however, has two problems.

First, Israeli politics is in gridlock. Olmert remains as prime minister even after the disaster in Lebanon in 2006, because no real successor has emerged. The operant concept of the Israelis is that the Palestinians are unstable and unpredictable. Any territorial concession made to the Palestinians — regardless of current interest or ideology — could ultimately be used against Israel. So, creating a Palestinian state in the West Bank would turn what is a good idea now into a geopolitical disaster later, should Abbas be succeeded by some of the more radical members of the al-Aqsa Martyrs Brigade — a group that carried out suicide bombings during the intifada. Israel's obsession with the unpredictability of the Palestinians and its belief in territorial buffers cannot be overcome by a weak government. Thirty years ago, it took Menachem Begin, heading a strong government from the right, to make peace with the Egyptians.

At the same time, the Israelis are terrified by the idea that Hamas will topple Fatah and take control of the Palestinian community as a whole. As Olmert was quoted as saying Nov. 23, "We cannot maintain the status quo between us and the Palestinians ... it will lead to results that are much worse that those of a failed conference. It will result in Hamas taking over Judea and Samaria, to a weakening or even the disappearance of the moderate Palestinians. Unless a political horizon can be found, the results will be deadly." Olmert clearly understands the stakes, but with Benjamin Netanyahu to his right, it is unclear whether he has the political weight to act on his perception.

For Olmert to make the kind of concessions that are needed in order to take advantage of the geopolitical situation, he needs one thing: guarantees and controls over the evolution of Hamas. We have seen Fatah go from what the Israelis consider the devil incarnate to a moderating force. Things change. If Hamas can be brought into the political process — and the split between Gaza and the West Bank maintained — Israel will be in a superb position. But who can moderate Hamas, and why would Hamas moderate?

Enter the Saudis. The Arab League resolution gave them cover for attending the Annapolis talks — which is the reason they engineered it. And the Saudis are the one force that has serious leverage with Hamas, because they underwrite much of Hamas' operations. Hamas is a Sunni Islamist group and, as such, has a sympathetic audience in Riyadh. Indeed, in many ways, Hamas is the Saudi answer to the secular Fatah. Therefore, if anyone can ultimately deliver Hamas, it would be the Saudis. But why would they?

On the surface, the Saudis should celebrate a radical, Islamist Palestinian movement, and on the surface they do. But they have become extremely wary of radical Islamism. Al Qaeda had a great deal of sympathy in the kingdom, but the evolution of events in the Islamic world since 9/11 is far from what the Saudis wanted to see. Islamist movements have created chaos from Pakistan to Lebanon, and this has created opportunities for a dangerous growth in Shiite power, not to mention that it has introduced U.S. forces into the region in the most destabilizing way possible.

At the end of the day, the Saudis and the other royal families in the Persian Gulf are profoundly conservative. They are wealthy — and become wildly wealthier every day, what with oil at more than $90 a barrel — and they have experienced dangerous instability inside the kingdom from al Qaeda and other radical Islamist movements. The Saudis have learned how difficult it is for the state to manage radical Islamism, and the way in which moral (and other) support for radicals can destabilize not only the region, but Saudi Arabia as well. Support in parts of the royal family for radical Islamist movements seems dicier to everyone now. These are movements that are difficult to control.

Most important, these are movements that fail. Persistently, these radical movements have not taken control of states and moved them in directions that align with Saudi interests. Rather, these movements have destabilized states, creating vacuums into which other movements can enter. The rise of Iranian power is particularly disturbing to the

Saudis, though so is the persistent presence of U.S. forces. A general calming of the situation is now in the Saudi interest. That means that the Saudi view of Hamas is somewhat different today than it was 10 years ago, when Riyadh was encouraging the group. A civil war among the Palestinians would achieve nothing. Nor, from the Saudi perspective, would another intifada, which would give the Americans more reason to act aggressively in the region. The Saudis have moved closer to the Americans and do not want them to withdraw from Iraq, for example, though they do wish the Americans would be less noisy. A Hamas grab for power in the West Bank is not something the Saudis want to see now.

Simply by participating in the Annapolis conference, the Saudis have signaled Hamas that they want a change of direction — although Hamas will resist. "The period that will follow the Annapolis conference will witness an increase of the resistance against the Zionist occupation in the West Bank and Gaza Strip," said Mussa Abu Marzuq, top aide to Hamas leader Khaled Meshaal. Perhaps, but a confrontation with the Saudis is not something that Hamas can afford now or in the future.

The Saudis want to stabilize the situation without destroying Hamas (which is very different from al Qaeda, given that it stems from the Muslim Brotherhood tradition). The Israelis want to maintain the split between Hamas and Fatah and limit Hamas' power without eliminating it — they like Fatah looking toward the Israelis for protection. Fatah badly needs to deliver concessions from Israel to strengthen its hand. The Americans can use a success and a change of atmospherics in the region.

Here is the delicate balance: Abbas has to receive more than he gives. Otherwise his credibility is shot. The Israelis find it difficult to make concessions, particularly disproportionate ones, with a weak government. But there are different kinds of strengths. Begin could make disproportionate concessions to the Egyptians because of his decisive political strength. Olmert is powerful only by default, though that is a kind of power.

It is interesting to think of how Ariel Sharon would have handled this situation. In a way he created it. By insisting that Israel withdraw from Gaza, he set in motion the split in the Palestinian community and the current dynamic. Had he not had his stroke, he would have tried to make Annapolis as defining a moment as the Begin-Sadat summit. It would be a risky move, but it should be recalled that few besides Begin believed that the Camp David Accords on the Sinai would have lasted 30 years. But that is merely editorializing. The facts on the ground indicate an opportunity to redefine the politics of the region. There are many factors lining up for it, the concessions Olmert would need to make in order to box Hamas in might simply be beyond his ability.

So long as no one mentions the status of Jerusalem, which blew up the Camp David meetings under Clinton, there is, nevertheless, a chance here — one we take more seriously than others.

The Palestinian Disconnect
June 19, 2007

Last week, an important thing happened in the Middle East. Hamas, a radical Islamist political group, forcibly seized control of Gaza from rival Fatah, an essentially secular Palestinian group. The West Bank, meanwhile, remains more or less under the control of Fatah, which dominates the Palestinian National Authority in that region. Therefore, for the first time, the two distinct Palestinian territories — the Gaza Strip and the West Bank — no longer are under a single Palestinian authority.

Hamas has been increasing its influence among the Palestinians for years, and it got a major boost by winning the most recent election. It now has claimed exclusive control over Gaza, its historical stronghold and power base. It is not clear whether Hamas will try to take control of the West Bank as well, or whether it would succeed if it did make such a play. The West Bank is a different region with a very different dynamic. What is certain, for the moment at least, is that these regions are divided under two factions, and therefore have the potential to become two different Palestinian states.

In a way, this makes more sense than the previous arrangement. The West Bank and the Gaza Strip are physically separated from one another by Israel. Travel from one part of the Palestinian territories to the other relies on Israel's willingness to permit it — which is not always forthcoming. As a result, the Palestinian territories are divided into two areas that have limited contact.

The war between the Philistines and the Hebrews is described in the books of Samuel. The Philistines controlled the coastal lowlands of the Levant, the east coast of the Mediterranean. They had advanced technologies, such as the ability to smelt bronze, and they conducted international trade up and down the Levant and within the eastern Mediterranean. The Hebrews, unable to engage the Philistines in direct combat, retreated into the hills to the east of the coast, in Judea, the area now called the West Bank.

The Philistines were part of a geographical entity that ran from Gaza north to Turkey. The Hebrews were part of the interior that connected north to Syria, south into the Arabian deserts and east across the Jordan. The Philistines were unable to pursue the Hebrews in the interior, and the Hebrews — until David — were unable to dislodge the Philistines from the coast. Two distinct entities existed.

Today, Gaza is tied to the coastal system, which Israel and Lebanon now occupy. Gaza is the link between the Levantine coast and Egypt. The West Bank is not a coastal entity but a region whose ties are to the Arabian Peninsula, Jordan and Syria. The point is that Gaza and the West Bank are very distinct geographical entities that see the world in very different ways.

Gaza, its links to the north cut by the Israelis, historically has been oriented toward the Egyptians, who occupied the region until 1967. The Egyptians influenced the region by creating the Palestine Liberation Organization, while its dissident Muslim Brotherhood helped influence the creation of Hamas in 1987. The West Bank, part of Jordan until 1967, is larger and more complex in its social organization, and it really represented the center of gravity of

Palestinian nationalism under Fatah. Gaza and the West Bank were always separate entities, and the recent action by Hamas has driven home that point.

Hamas' victory in Gaza means much more to the Palestinians and Egyptians than it does to the Israelis — at least in the shorter term. The fear in Israel now is that Gaza, under Hamas, will become more aggressive in carrying out terrorist attacks in Israel. Hamas certainly has an ideology that argues for this, and it is altogether possible that the group will become more antagonistic. However, it appears to us that Hamas already was capable of carrying out as many attacks as it wished before taking complete control. Moreover, by increasing attacks now, Hamas — which always has been able to deny responsibility for these incidents — would lose the element of deniability. Having taken control of Gaza, regardless of whether it carries out attacks, it would have failed to prevent them. Hamas' leadership is more vulnerable now than ever before.

Let's consider the strategic position of the Palestinians. Their primary weapon against Israel remains what it always has been: random attacks against civilian targets designed to destabilize Israel. The problem with this strategy is obvious. Using terrorism against Americans in Iraq is potentially effective as a strategy. If the Americans cannot stand the level of casualties being imposed, they have the option of leaving Iraq. Although leaving might pose serious problems to U.S. regional and global interests, it would not affect the continued existence of the United States. Therefore, the insurgents potentially could find a threshold that would force the United States to fold.

The Israelis cannot leave Israel. Assume for the moment that the Palestinians could impose 1,000 civilian casualties a year. There are about 5 million Jews in Israel. That would be about 0.02 percent casualties. The Israelis are not gong to leave Israel at that casualty rate, or at a rate a thousand times greater. Unlike the Americans, for whom Iraq is a subsidiary interest, Israel is Israel's central interest. Israel is not going to capitulate to the Palestinians over terrorism attacks.

The Israelis could be convinced to make political concessions in shaping a Palestinian state. For example, they might concede more land or more autonomy in order to stop the attacks. That might have been attractive to Fatah, but Hamas explicitly rejects the existence of Israel and therefore gives the Israelis no reason to make concessions. That means that while attacks might be psychologically satisfying to Hamas, they would be substantially less effective than the attacks that were carried out while Fatah was driving the negotiations. Bargaining with Hamas gets Israel nothing.

One of the uses of terrorism is to trigger an Israeli response, which in turn can be used to drive a wedge between Israel and the West. Fatah has been historically skillful at using the cycle of violence to its political advantage. Hamas, however, is handicapped in two ways: First, its position on Israel is perceived as much less reasonable than Fatah's. Second, Hamas is increasingly being viewed as a jihadist movement, and, as such, its strength threatens European and U.S. interests.

Although Israel does not want terrorist attacks, such attacks do not represent a threat to the survival of the state. To be cold-blooded, they are an irritant, not a strategic threat.

The only thing that could threaten the survival of Israel, apart from a nuclear barrage, would be a shift in position of neighboring states. Right now, Israel has peace treaties with both Egypt and Jordan, and an adequately working relationship with Syria. With Egypt and Jordan out of the game, Syria does not represent a threat. Israel is strategically secure.

The single most important neighbor Israel has is Egypt. When energized, it is the center of gravity of the Arab world. Under former President Gamal Abdul Nasser, Egypt drove Arab hostility to Israel. Once Anwar Sadat reversed Nasser's strategy on Israel, the Jewish state was basically secure. Other Arab nations could not threaten it unless Egypt was part of the equation. And for nearly 30 years, Egypt has not been part of the equation. But if Egypt were to reverse its position, Israel would, over time, find itself much less comfortable. Though Saudi Arabia has recently overshadowed Egypt's role in the Arab world, the Egyptians can always opt back into a strong leadership position and use their strength to threaten Israel. This becomes especially important as Egyptian President Hosni Mubarak's health fails and questions are raised about whether his successors will be able to maintain control of the country while the Muslim Brotherhood spearheads a campaign to demand political reform.

As we have said, Gaza is part of the Mediterranean coastal system. Egypt controlled Gaza until 1967 and retained influence there afterward, but not in the West Bank. Hamas also was influenced by Egypt, but not by Mubarak's government. Hamas was an outgrowth of the Egyptian Muslim Brotherhood, which the Mubarak regime has done a fairly good job of containing, primarily through force. But there also is a significant paradox in Hamas' relations with Egypt. The Mubarak regime, particularly through its intelligence chief (and prospective Mubarak successor) Omar Suleiman, has good working relations with Hamas, despite being tough on the Muslim Brotherhood.

This is the threat to Israel. Hamas has ties to Egypt and resonates with Egyptians, as well as with Saudis. Its members are religious Sunnis. If the creation of an Islamist Palestinian state in Gaza succeeds, the most important blowback might be in Egypt, where the Muslim Brotherhood — which is currently lying very low — could be rekindled. Mubarak is growing old, and he hopes to be succeeded by his son. The credibility of the regime is limited, to say the least.

Hamas is unlikely to take over the West Bank — and, even if it did, it still would make no strategic difference. Increased terrorist attacks against Israel's population would achieve less than the attacks that occurred while Fatah was negotiating. They could happen, but they would lead nowhere. Hamas' long-term strategy — indeed, the only hope of the Palestinians who are not prepared to accept a compromise with Israel — is for Egypt to change its tune toward Israel, which could very well involve energizing Islamist forces in Egypt and bringing about the fall of the Mubarak regime. That is the key to any solution for Hamas.

Although many are focusing on the rise of Iran's influence in Gaza, putting aside the rhetoric, Iran is a minor player in the Israeli-Palestinian equation. Even Syria, despite hosting Hamas' exiled leadership, carries little weight when it comes to posing a strategic threat to Israel. But Egypt carries enormous weight. If an Islamist rising occurred in Egypt and a regime was installed that could energize the Egyptian public against Israel, then that would reflect a strategic threat to the survival of the Israeli state. It would not be an immediate threat — it would take a generation to turn Egypt into a military power — but it would ultimately represent a threat.

Only a disciplined and hostile Egypt could serve as the cornerstone of an anti-Israel coalition. Hamas, by asserting itself in Gaza — especially if it can resist the Israeli army — could strike the chord in Egypt that Fatah has been unable to strike for almost 30 years.

That is the importance of the creation of a separate Gaza entity; it complicates Israeli-Palestinian negotiations, and probably makes them impossible. And this in and of itself works in Israel's favor, since it has no need to even entertain negotiations with the Palestinians as long as the Palestinians continue dividing themselves. If Hamas were to make significant inroads in the West Bank, it would make things more difficult for Israel, as well as for Jordan. But with or without the West Bank, Hamas has the potential — not the certainty, just the potential — to reach west along the Mediterranean coast and influence events in Egypt. And that is the key for Hamas.

There are probably a dozen reasons why Hamas made the move it did, most of them trivial and limited to local problems. But the strategic consequence of an independent, Islamist Gaza is that it can act both as a symbol and as a catalyst for change in Egypt, something that was difficult as long as Hamas was entangled with the West Bank. This probably was not planned, but it is certainly the most important consequence — intended or not — of the Gaza affair.

Two things must be monitored: first, whether there is reconciliation between Gaza and the West Bank and, if so, on what sort of terms; second, what the Egyptian Islamists led by the Muslim Brotherhood do now that Hamas, its own creation, has taken control of Gaza, a region once controlled by the Egyptians.

Egypt is the place to watch.

CHAPTER 5: Israeli Decisions and the Broader World

Politics Over Geopolitics
Oct. 1, 2007

Israeli Prime Minister Ehud Olmert and Palestinian President Mahmoud Abbas will meet Oct. 2 for the sixth summit in the current peace process, leading up to an international peace conference planned by the United States for November. Normally, such peace conferences either achieve nothing or culminate in disaster. In the first case, they are simply gestures by all sides toward a peace process, without anyone really expecting a resolution. They are PR moves.

Then there are summits that really tackle fundamental tensions, like then-U.S. President Bill Clinton's Camp David meeting in 2000 with Ehud Barak and Yasser Arafat. At these kinds of meetings, core issues — such as the status of Palestinian refugees, control of Jerusalem and recognition of Israel's right to exist — are faced squarely. Either the meeting blows apart on the spot, or the two sides start making concessions, in which case there are explosions back home. Normally, neither side has the political authority to make concessions; so with the grand gestures over, everyone goes home after the photo-ops are completed and life goes on pretty much as it did before.

The great exception to this rule was the Camp David Accords signed between Egypt and Israel 30 years ago. In spite of universal expectations to the contrary, that agreement has held for more than a generation. It is the foundation of Israeli national security — since a serious conventional threat to Israel is impossible without Egypt's participation — and it relieved Egypt of the burden of confronting Israel. It was an agreement rooted in geopolitical reality. Egypt did not wish to mortgage its future on behalf of the Palestinians and the Israelis did not need the Sinai desert. A buffer zone was created, with foreign troops symbolically enforcing the buffer — and it worked.

For any Israeli-Palestinian agreement to have any chance of working, there has to be some geopolitical rationality to it. Up to now, no settlement has been possible because of geography. A Palestinian state on the West Bank and Gaza is a social and economic abortion. It would immediately fall into dependence on Israel. Yet, at the same time, it represents a long-term threat to Israeli security, creating a Palestinian state within artillery range of Tel Aviv. And this does not even begin to deal with the questions of the future of Jerusalem, the right of Palestinians to return to Israel, or compensation for Israelis who left Arab countries.

But there is an opening at the moment. The victory of Hamas in Gaza and the continuation of the Palestinian National Authority in the West Bank has, for the moment, effectively created two Palestinian entities. In many ways, they are more bitterly opposed to each other than they are to

Israel, at least for the time being. The division of the Palestinians is obviously advantageous to the Israelis.

Now the Israelis have to make a strategic decision. The maintenance of a split among the Palestinians requires that Abbas be strengthened. Israel is releasing Fatah fighters from prisons to bolster Abbas' forces. But creating a political settlement with Abbas that leaves Hamas stranded and isolated in Gaza, while Abbas' West Bank entity emerges into as viable a state as possible, is more difficult and more important. It means that Israel must deal with the more intractable issues, making concessions not only to strengthen secular Palestinians against Islamists but also to institutionalize the split in the Palestinian community.

The kind of political settlement that has to be made to strengthen Abbas will run directly into Israeli domestic politics. Fatah was the sponsor of the al-Aqsa Martyrs Brigade, which was pivotal in the suicide bombing campaigns. Abbas has common interests with Israel for the moment, but he is no friend of Israel by any stretch of the imagination. For many Israelis, Abbas is the heir of Arafat, which means the heir of 40 years of terrorism.

Olmert hardly has the political base to make concessions to Abbas. At the same time, the deep division among the Palestinians, which has always been there in various ways, has now congealed into a geographical split. The more radical and intractable faction controls Gaza. Its enemy, the more secular movement, dominates the West Bank. The West Bank is far more important to Israel than Gaza. Maintaining that split and making a separate peace with Abbas should be tantalizing.

But the Israelis are likely to pass up the chance, for three reasons. First, they simply don't trust Abbas. Second, a Palestinian state along the 1948 borders poses a danger to Israel whether or not it includes Gaza. Finally, the Israelis are not prepared to make the kind of concessions that would make Abbas a Palestinian hero. However, from the Israeli point of view, the problem with inaction is that Hamas has been the rising tide among Palestinians — if Israel passes on this moment, it could face Hamas in a pre-eminent position in the West Bank as well as in Gaza.

Splitting one's enemies is the pivot of geopolitics. The United States sided with Stalin against Hitler, with Mao against Brezhnev. The Palestinians have split themselves. Geopolitically, Israel has an obvious move, but politically it is an unsustainable one. Abbas is no friend of Israel and is playing his own game. His back is against the wall. But Abbas has a common enemy with Israel: Hamas.

It is Israel's move. If history is any guide, it will choose politics over geopolitics.

The Geopolitics of the U.S.-Israeli Relationship
Sept. 4, 2007

U.S. President George W. Bush made an appearance in Iraq's restive Anbar province on Sept. 3 — in part to tout the success of the military surge there ahead of the presentation in Washington of the Petraeus report. For the next month or two, the battle over Iraq will be waged in Washington — and one country will come up over and over again, from any number of directions: Israel. Israel will be invoked as an ally in the war on terrorism — the reason the United States is in the war in the first place. Some will say that Israel maneuvered the United States into Iraq to serve its own purposes. Some will say it orchestrated 9/11 for its own ends. Others will say that, had the United States supported Israel more resolutely, there would not have been a 9/11.

There is probably no relationship on which people have more diverging views than on that between the United States and Israel. Therefore, since it is going to be invoked in the coming weeks — and Bush is taking a fairly irrelevant pause at the Asia-Pacific Economic Cooperation summit in Australia — this is an opportune time to consider the geopolitics of the U.S.-Israeli relationship.

Let's begin with some obvious political points. There is a relatively small Jewish community in the United States, though its political influence is magnified by its strategic location in critical states such as New York and the fact that it is more actively involved in politics than some other ethnic groups.

The Jewish community, as tends to be the case with groups, is deeply divided on many issues. It tends to be united on one issue — Israel — but not with the same intensity as in the past, nor with even a semblance of agreement on the specifics. The American Jewish community is as divided as the Israeli Jewish community, with a large segment of people who don't much care thrown in. At the same time, this community donates large sums of money to American and Israeli organizations, including groups that lobby on behalf of Israeli issues in Washington. These lobbying entities lean toward the right wing of Israel's political spectrum, in large part because the Israeli right has tended to govern in the past generation and these groups tend to follow the dominant Israeli strand. It also is because American Jews who contribute to Israel lobby organizations lean right in both Israeli and American politics.

The Israel lobby, which has a great deal of money and experience, is extremely influential in Washington. For decades now, it has done a good job of ensuring that Israeli interests are attended to in Washington, and certainly on some issues it has skewed U.S. policy on the Middle East. There are Jews who practice being shocked at this assertion, but they must not be taken seriously. They know better, which is why they donate money. Others pretend to be shocked at the idea of a lobbyist influencing U.S. policy on the Middle East, but they also need not be taken seriously, because they are trying to influence Washington as well, though they are not as successful. Obviously there is an influential Israel lobby in Washington.

There are, however, two important questions. The first is whether this is in any way unique. Is a strong Israel lobby an unprecedented intrusion into foreign policy? The key question, though, is whether Israeli interests diverge from U.S. interests to the extent that the Israel lobby is taking U.S. foreign policy in directions it wouldn't go otherwise, in directions that counter the U.S. national interest.

Begin with the first question. Prior to both world wars there was extensive debate on whether the United States should intervene in the war. In both cases, the British government lobbied extensively for U.S. intervention on behalf of the United Kingdom. The British made two arguments. The first was that the United States shared a heritage with England — code for the idea that white Anglo-Saxon Protestants should stand with white Anglo-Saxon Protestants. The second was that there was a fundamental political affinity between British and U.S. democracy and that it was in the U.S. interest to protect British democracy from German authoritarianism.

Many Americans, including President Franklin Roosevelt, believed both arguments. The British lobby was quite powerful. There was a German lobby as well, but it lacked the numbers, the money and the traditions to draw on.

From a geopolitical point of view, both arguments were weak. The United States and the United Kingdom not only were separate countries, they had fought some bitter wars over the question. As for political institutions, geopolitics, as a method, is fairly insensitive to the moral claims of regimes. It works on the basis of interest. On that basis, an intervention on behalf of the United Kingdom in both wars made sense because it provided a relatively low-cost way of preventing Germany from dominating Europe and challenging American sea power. In the end, it wasn't the lobbying interest, massive though it was, but geopolitical necessity that drove U.S. intervention.

The second question, then, is: Has the Israel lobby caused the United States to act in ways that contravene U.S. interests? For example, by getting the United States to support Israel, did it turn the Arab world against the Americans? Did it support Israeli repression of Palestinians, and thereby generate an Islamist radicalism that led to 9/11? Did it manipulate U.S. policy on Iraq so that the United

States invaded Iraq on behalf of Israel? These allegations have all been made. If true, they are very serious charges.

It is important to remember that U.S.-Israeli ties were not extraordinarily close prior to 1967. President Harry Truman recognized Israel, but the United States had not provided major military aid and support. Israel, always in need of an outside supply of weapons, first depended on the Soviet Union, which shipped weapons to Israel via Czechoslovakia. When the Soviets realized that Israeli socialists were anti-Soviet as well, they dropped Israel. Israel's next patron was France. France was fighting to hold on to Algeria and maintain its influence in Lebanon and Syria, both former French protectorates. The French saw Israel as a natural ally. It was France that really created the Israeli air force and provided the first technology for Israeli nuclear weapons.

The United States was actively hostile to Israel during this period. In 1956, following Gamal Abdul Nasser's seizure of power in Egypt, Cairo nationalized the Suez Canal. Without the canal, the British Empire was finished, and ultimately the French were as well. The United Kingdom and France worked secretly with Israel, and Israel invaded the Sinai. Then, in order to protect the Suez Canal from an Israeli-Egyptian war, a Franco-British force parachuted in to seize the canal. President Dwight Eisenhower forced the British and French to withdraw — as well as the Israelis. U.S.-Israeli relations remained chilly for quite a while.

The break point with France came in 1967. The Israelis, under pressure from Egypt, decided to invade Egypt, Jordan and Syria — ignoring French President Charles de Gaulle's demand that they not do so. As a result, France broke its alignment with Israel. This was the critical moment in U.S.-Israeli relations. Israel needed a source of weaponry as its national security needs vastly outstripped its industrial base. It was at this point that the Israeli lobby in the United States became critical. Israel wanted a relationship with the United States and the Israeli lobby brought tremendous pressure to bear, picturing Israel as a heroic, embattled democracy, surrounded by bloodthirsty neighbors, badly needing U.S. help. President Lyndon B. Johnson, bogged down in Vietnam and wanting to shore up his base, saw a popular cause in Israel and tilted toward it.

But there were critical strategic issues as well. Syria and Iraq had both shifted into the pro-Soviet camp, as had Egypt. Some have argued that, had the United States not supported Israel, this would not have happened. This, however, runs in the face of history. It was the United States that forced the Israelis out of the Sinai in 1956, but the Egyptians moved into the Soviet camp anyway. The argument that it was uncritical support for Israel that caused anti-Americanism in the Arab world doesn't hold water. The Egyptians became anti-American in spite of an essentially anti-Israeli position in 1956. By 1957 Egypt was a Soviet ally.

The Americans ultimately tilted toward Israel because of this, not the other way around. Egypt was not only providing the Soviets with naval and air bases, it also was running covert operations in the Arabian Peninsula to bring down the conservative sheikhdoms there, including Saudi Arabia's. The Soviets were seen as using Egypt as a base of operations against the United States. Syria was seen as another dangerous radical power, along with Iraq. The defense of the Arabian Peninsula from radical, pro-Soviet Arab movements, as well as the defense of Jordan, became a central interest of the United States.

Israel was seen as contributing by threatening the security of both Egypt and Syria. The Saudi fear of the Palestine Liberation Organization (PLO) was palpable. Riyadh saw the Soviet-inspired liberation movements as threatening Saudi Arabia's survival. Israel was engaged in a covert war against the PLO and related groups, and that was exactly what the Saudis wanted from the late 1960s until the early 1980s. Israel's covert capability against the PLO, coupled with its overt military power against Egypt and Syria, was very much in the American interest and that of its Arab allies. It was a low-cost solution to some very difficult strategic problems at a time when the United States was either in Vietnam or recovering from the war.

The occupation of the Sinai, the West Bank and the Golan Heights in 1967 was not in the U.S. interest. The United States wanted Israel to carry out its mission against Soviet-backed paramilitaries and tie down Egypt and Syria, but the occupation was not seen as part of that mission. The Israelis initially expected to convert their occupation of the territories into a peace treaty, but that only happened, much later, with Egypt. At the Khartoum summit in 1967, the Arabs delivered the famous three noes: No negotiation. No recognition. No peace. Israel became an occupying power. It has never found its balance.

The claim has been made that if the United States forced the Israelis out of the West Bank and Gaza, then it would receive credit and peace would follow. There are three problems with that theory. First, the Israelis did not occupy these areas prior to 1967 and there was no peace. Second, groups such as Hamas and Hezbollah have said that a withdrawal would not end the state of war with Israel. And therefore, third, the withdrawal would create friction with Israel without any clear payoff from the Arabs. It must be remembered that Egypt and Jordan have both signed peace treaties with Israel and seem not to care one whit about the Palestinians. The Saudis have never risked a thing for the Palestinians, nor have the Iranians. The Syrians have, but they are far more interested in investing in Beirut hotels than in invading Israel. No Arab state is interested in the Palestinians, except for those that are actively hostile. There is Arab and Islamic public opinion and nonstate organizations, but none would be satisfied with an Israeli withdrawal. They want Israel destroyed. Even if the United States withdrew all support for Israel, however, Israel would not be destroyed. The radical Arabs do not want withdrawal; they want destruction. And the moderate Arabs don't care about the Palestinians beyond rhetoric.

Now we get to the heart of the matter. If the United States broke ties with Israel, would the U.S. geopolitical position be improved? In other words, if it broke with Israel, would Iran or al Qaeda come to view the United States in a different way? Critics of the Israel lobby argue that, except for U.S. support for Israel, the United States would have better relations in the Muslim world, and would not be targeted by al Qaeda or threatened by Iran. In other words, except for the Israeli lobby's influence, the United States would be much more secure.

Al Qaeda does not see Israel by itself as its central problem. Its goal is the resurrection of the caliphate — and it sees U.S. support for Muslim regimes as the central problem. If the United States abandoned Israel, al Qaeda would still confront U.S. support for countries such as Egypt, Saudi Arabia and Pakistan. For al Qaeda, Israel is an important issue, but for the United States to soothe al Qaeda, it would have to abandon not only Israel but also its non-Islamist allies in the Middle East.

As for Iran, the Iranian rhetoric, as we have said, has never been matched by action. During the Iran-Iraq War, the Iranian military purchased weapons and parts from the Israelis. It was more delighted than anyone when Israel destroyed the Iraqi nuclear reactor in 1981. Iran's problem with the United States is its presence in Iraq, its naval presence in the Persian Gulf and its support for the Kurds. If Israel disappeared from the face of the Earth, Iran's problems would remain the same.

It has been said that the Israelis inspired the U.S. invasion of Iraq. There is no doubt that Israel was pleased when, after 9/11, the United States saw itself as an anti-Islamist power. Let us remind our more creative readers, however, that benefiting from something does not mean you caused it. However, it has never been clear that the Israelis were all that enthusiastic about invading Iraq. Neoconservative Jews like Paul Wolfowitz were enthusiastic, as were non-Jews like Dick Cheney. But the Israeli view of a U.S. invasion of Iraq was at most mixed, and to some extent dubious. The Israelis liked the Iran-Iraq balance of power and were close allies of Turkey, which certainly opposed the invasion. The claim that Israel supported the invasion comes from those who mistake neoconservatives, many of whom are Jews who support

Israel, with Israeli foreign policy, which was much more nuanced than the neoconservatives. The Israelis were not at all clear about what the Americans were doing in Iraq, but they were in no position to complain.

Israeli-U.S. relations have gone through three phases. From 1948 to 1967, the United States supported Israel's right to exist but was not its patron. In the 1967-1991 period, the Israelis were a key American asset in the Cold War. From 1991 to the present, the relationship has remained close but it is not pivotal to either country. Washington cannot help Israel with Hezbollah or Hamas. The Israelis cannot help the United States in Iraq or Afghanistan. If the relationship were severed, it would have remarkably little impact on either country — though keeping the relationship is more valuable than severing it.

To sum up: There is a powerful Jewish, pro-Israel lobby in Washington, though it was not very successful in the first 20 years or so of Israel's history. When U.S. policy toward Israel swung in 1967 it had far more to do with geopolitical interests than with lobbying. The United States needed help with Egypt and Syria and Israel could provide it. Lobbying appeared to be the key, but it wasn't; geopolitical necessity was. Egypt was anti-American even when the United States was anti-Israeli. Al Qaeda would be anti-American even if the United States were anti-Israel. Rhetoric aside, Iran has never taken direct action against Israel and has much more important things on its plate.

Portraying the Israeli lobby as super-powerful behooves two groups: Critics of U.S. Middle Eastern policy and the Israel lobby itself. Critics get to say the U.S. relationship with Israel is the result of manipulation and corruption. Thus, they get to avoid discussing the actual history of Israel, the United States and the Middle East. The lobby benefits from having robust power because one of its jobs is to raise funds — and the image of a killer lobby opens a lot more pocketbooks than does the idea that both Israel and the United States are simply pursuing their geopolitical interests and that things would go on pretty much the same even without slick lobbying.

The great irony is that the critics of U.S. policy and the Israeli lobby both want to believe in the same myth — that great powers can be manipulated to harm themselves by crafty politicians. The British didn't get the United States into the world wars, and the Israelis aren't maneuvering the Americans into being pro-Israel. Beyond its ability to exert itself on small things, the Israeli lobby is powerful in influencing Washington to do what it is going to do anyway. What happens next in Iraq is not up to the Israeli lobby — though it and the Saudi Embassy have a different story.

Israeli Strategy After the Russo-Georgian War
Sept. 8, 2008

The Russo-Georgian war continues to resonate, and it is time to expand our view of it. The primary players in Georgia, apart from the Georgians, were the Russians and Americans. On the margins were the Europeans, providing advice and admonitions but carrying little weight. Another player, carrying out a murkier role, was Israel. Israeli advisers were present in Georgia alongside American advisers, and Israeli businessmen were doing business there. The Israelis had a degree of influence but were minor players compared to the Americans.

More interesting, perhaps, was the decision, publicly announced by the Israelis, to end weapons sales to Georgia the week before the Georgians attacked South Ossetia. Clearly the Israelis knew what was coming and wanted no part of it. Afterward, unlike the Americans, the Israelis did everything they could to placate the Russians, including having Israeli Prime Minister Ehud Olmert travel to Moscow to offer reassurances. Whatever the Israelis were doing in Georgia, they did not want a confrontation with the Russians.

It is impossible to explain the Israeli reasoning for being in Georgia outside the context of a careful review of Israeli strategy in general. From that, we can begin to understand why the Israelis are involved in affairs far outside their immediate area of responsibility, and why they responded the way they did in Georgia.

We need to divide Israeli strategic interests into four separate but interacting pieces:

- The Palestinians living inside Israel's post-1967 borders.

- The so-called "confrontation states" that border Israel, including Lebanon, Syria, Jordan and especially Egypt.

- The Muslim world beyond this region.

- The great powers able to influence and project power into these first three regions.

The Palestinian Issue

The most important thing to understand about the first interest, the Palestinian issue, is that the Palestinians do not represent a strategic threat to the Israelis. Their ability to inflict casualties is an irritant to the Israelis (if a tragedy to the victims and their families), but they cannot threaten the existence of the Israeli state. The Palestinians can impose a level of irritation that can affect Israeli morale, inducing the Israelis to make concessions based on the realistic assessment that the Palestinians by themselves cannot in any conceivable time frame threaten Israel's core interests, regardless of political arrangements. At the same time, the argument goes, given that the Palestinians cannot threaten Israeli interests, what is the value of making concessions that will not change the threat of terrorist attacks? Given the structure of Israeli politics, this matter is both substrategic and gridlocked.

The matter is compounded by the fact that the Palestinians are deeply divided among themselves. For Israel, this is a benefit, as it creates a de facto civil war among Palestinians and reduces the threat from them. But it also reduces pressure and opportunities to negotiate. There is no one on the Palestinian side who speaks authoritatively for all Palestinians. Any agreement reached with the Palestinians would, from the Israeli point of view, have to include guarantees on the cessation of terrorism. No one has ever been in a position to guarantee that — and certainly Fatah does not today speak for Hamas. Therefore, a settlement on a Palestinian state remains gridlocked because it does not deliver any meaningful advantages to the Israelis.

The Confrontation States

The second area involves the confrontation states. Israel has formal peace treaties with Egypt and Jordan. It has had informal understandings with Damascus on things like Lebanon, but Israel has no permanent understanding with Syria. The Lebanese are too deeply divided to allow state-to-state understandings, but Israel has had understandings with different Lebanese factions at different times (and particularly close relations with some of the Christian factions).

Jordan is effectively an ally of Israel. It has been hostile to the Palestinians at least since 1970, when the Palestine Liberation Organization attempted to overthrow the Hashemite regime, and the Jordanians regard the Israelis and Americans as guarantors of their national security. Israel's relationship with Egypt is publicly cooler but quite cooperative. The only group that poses any serious challenge to the Egyptian state is The Muslim Brotherhood, and hence Cairo views Hamas — a derivative of that organization — as a potential threat. The Egyptians and Israelis have maintained peaceful relations for more than 30 years, regardless of the state of Israeli-Palestinian relations. The Syrians by themselves cannot go to war with Israel and survive. Their primary interest lies in Lebanon, and when they work against Israel, they work with surrogates like Hezbollah. But their own view on an independent Palestinian state is murky, since they claim all of Palestine as part of a greater Syria — a view not particularly relevant at the moment. Therefore, Israel's only threat on its border comes from Syria via surrogates in Lebanon and the possibility of Syria's acquiring weaponry that would threaten Israel, such as chemical or nuclear weapons.

The Wider Muslim World

As to the third area, Israel's position in the Muslim world beyond the confrontation states is much more secure than either it or its enemies would like to admit. Israel has close, formal strategic relations with Turkey as well as with Morocco. Turkey and Egypt are the giants of the region, and being aligned with them provides Israel with the foundations of regional security. But Israel also has excellent relations with countries where formal relations do not exist, particularly in the Arabian Peninsula.

The conservative monarchies of the region deeply distrust the Palestinians, particularly Fatah. As part of the Nasserite Pan-Arab socialist movement, Fatah on several occasions directly threatened these monarchies. Several times in the 1970s and 1980s, Israeli intelligence provided these monarchies with information that prevented assassinations or uprisings.

Saudi Arabia, for one, has never engaged in anti-Israeli activities beyond rhetoric. In the aftermath of the 2006 Israeli-Hezbollah conflict, Saudi Arabia and Israel forged close behind-the-scenes relations, especially because of an assertive Iran — a common foe of both the Saudis and the Israelis. Saudi Arabia has close relations with Hamas, but these have as much to do with maintaining a defensive position — keeping Hamas and its Saudi backers off Riyadh's back — as they do with government policy. The Saudis are cautious regarding Hamas, and the other monarchies are even more so.

More to the point, Israel does extensive business with these regimes, particularly in the defense area. Israeli companies, working formally through American or European subsidiaries, carry out extensive business throughout the Arabian Peninsula. The nature of these subsidiaries is well-known on all sides, though no one is eager to trumpet this. The governments of both Israel and the Arabian Peninsula would have internal political problems if they publicized it, but a visit to Dubai, the business capital of the region, would find many Israelis doing extensive business under third-party passports. Add to this that the states of the Arabian Peninsula are afraid of Iran, and the relationship becomes even more important to all sides.

There is an interesting idea that if Israel were to withdraw from the occupied territories and create an independent Palestinian state, then perceptions of Israel in the Islamic world would shift. This is a commonplace view in Europe. The fact is that we can divide the Muslim world into three groups.

First, there are those countries that already have formal ties to Israel. Second are those that have close working relations with Israel and where formal ties would complicate rather than deepen relations. Pakistan and Indonesia, among others, fit into this class. Third are those that are absolutely hostile to Israel, such as Iran. It is very difficult to identify a state that has no informal or formal relations with Israel but would adopt these relations if there were a Palestinian state. Those states that are hostile to Israel would remain hostile after a withdrawal from the Palestinian territories, since their issue is with the existence of Israel, not its borders.

The point of all this is that Israeli security is much better than it might appear if one listened only to the rhetoric. The Palestinians are divided and at war with each other. Under the best of circumstances, they cannot threaten Israel's survival. The only bordering countries with which the Israelis have no formal agreements are Syria and Lebanon, and neither can threaten Israel's security. Israel has close ties to Turkey, the most powerful Muslim country in the region. It also has much closer commercial and intelligence ties with the Arabian Peninsula than is generally acknowledged, although the degree of cooperation is well-known in the region. From a security standpoint, Israel is doing well.

The Broader World

Israel is also doing extremely well in the broader world, the fourth and final area. Israel always has needed a foreign source of weapons and technology, since its national security needs outstrip its domestic industrial capacity. Its first patron was the Soviet Union, which hoped to gain a foothold in the Middle East. This was quickly followed by France, which saw Israel as an ally in Algeria and against Egypt. Finally, after 1967, the United States came to support Israel. Washington saw Israel as a threat to Syria, which could threaten Turkey from the rear at a time when the Soviets were threatening Turkey from the north. Turkey was the doorway to the Mediterranean, and Syria was a threat to Turkey. Egypt was also aligned with the Soviets from 1956 onward, long before the United States had developed a close working relationship with Israel. That relationship has declined in importance for the Israelis. Over the years the amount of U.S. aid — roughly $2.5 billion annually — has remained relatively constant. It was never adjusted upward for inflation, and so shrunk as a percentage of Israeli gross domestic product from roughly 20 percent in 1974 to under 2 percent today. Israel's dependence on the United States has plummeted. The dependence that once existed has become a marginal convenience. Israel holds onto the aid less for economic reasons than to maintain the concept in the United States of Israeli dependence and U.S. responsibility for Israeli security. In other words, it is more psychological and political from Israel's point of view than an economic or security requirement.

Israel therefore has no threats or serious dependencies, save two. The first is the acquisition of nuclear weapons by a power that cannot be deterred — in other words, a nation prepared to commit suicide to destroy Israel. Given Iranian rhetoric, Iran would appear at times to be such a nation. But given that the Iranians are far from having a deliverable weapon, and that in the Middle East no one's rhetoric should be taken all that seriously, the Iranian threat is not one the Israelis are compelled to deal with right now.

The second threat would come from the emergence of a major power prepared to intervene overtly or covertly in the region for its own interests, and in the course of doing so, redefine the regional threat to Israel. The major candidate for this role is Russia.

During the Cold War, the Soviets pursued a strategy to undermine American interests in the region. In the course of this, the Soviets activated states and groups that could directly threaten Israel. There is no significant conventional military threat to Israel on its borders unless Egypt is willing and well-armed. Since the mid-1970s, Egypt has been neither. Even if Egyptian President Hosni Mubarak were to die and be replaced by a regime hostile to Israel, Cairo could do nothing unless it had a patron capable of training and arming its military. The same is true of Syria and Iran to a great extent. Without access to outside military technology, Iran is a nation merely of frightening press conferences. With access, the entire regional equation shifts.

After the fall of the Soviet Union, no one was prepared to intervene in the Middle East the way the Soviets had. The Chinese have absolutely no interest in struggling with the United States in the Middle East, which accounts for a similar percentage of Chinese and U.S. oil consumption. It is far cheaper to buy oil in the Middle East than to engage in a geopolitical struggle with China's major trade partner, the United States. Even if there was interest, no European powers can play this role given their individual military weakness, and Europe as a whole is a geopolitical myth. The only country that can threaten the balance of power in the Israeli geopolitical firmament is Russia.

Israel fears that if Russia gets involved in a struggle with the United States, Moscow will aid Middle Eastern regimes that are hostile to the United States as one of its levers, beginning with Syria and Iran. Far more frightening to the Israelis is the idea of the Russians once again playing a covert role in Egypt, toppling the tired Mubarak regime, installing one friendlier to their own interests, and arming it. Israel's fundamental fear is not Iran. It is a rearmed, motivated and hostile Egypt backed by a great power.

The Russians are not after Israel, which is a sideshow for them. But in the course of finding ways to threaten American interests in the Middle East — seeking to force the Americans out of their desired sphere of influence in the former Soviet region — the Russians could undermine what at the moment is a quite secure position in the Middle East for the United States.

This brings us back to what the Israelis were doing in Georgia. They were not trying to acquire airbases from which to bomb Iran. That would take thousands of Israeli personnel in Georgia for maintenance, munitions management, air traffic control and so on. And it would take Ankara allowing the use of Turkish airspace, which isn't very likely. Plus, if that were the plan, then stopping the Georgians from attacking South Ossetia would have been a logical move.

The Israelis were in Georgia in an attempt, in parallel with the United States, to prevent Russia's re-emergence as a great power. The nuts and bolts of that effort involves shoring up states in the former Soviet region that are hostile to Russia, as well as supporting individuals in Russia who oppose Prime Minister Vladimir Putin's direction. The Israeli presence in Georgia, like the American one, was designed to block the re-emergence of Russia.

ISRAELI DECISIONS AND THE BROADER WORLD

As soon as the Israelis got wind of a coming clash in South Ossetia, they — unlike the United States — switched policies dramatically. Where the United States increased its hostility toward Russia, the Israelis ended weapons sales to Georgia before the war. After the war, the Israelis initiated diplomacy designed to calm Russian fears. Indeed, at the moment the Israelis have a greater interest in keeping the Russians from seeing Israel as an enemy than they have in keeping the Americans happy. U.S. Vice President Dick Cheney may be uttering vague threats to the Russians. But Olmert was reassuring Moscow it has nothing to fear from Israel, and therefore should not sell weapons to Syria, Iran, Hezbollah or anyone else hostile to Israel.

Interestingly, the Americans have started pumping out information that the Russians are selling weapons to Hezbollah and Syria. The Israelis have avoided that issue carefully. They can live with some weapons in Hezbollah's hands a lot more easily than they can live with a coup in Egypt followed by the introduction of Russian military advisers. One is a nuisance; the other is an existential threat. Russia may not be in a position to act yet, but the Israelis aren't waiting for the situation to get out of hand.

Israel is in control of the Palestinian situation and relations with the countries along its borders. Its position in the wider Muslim world is much better than it might appear. Its only enemy there is Iran, and that threat is much less clear than the Israelis say publicly. But the threat of Russia intervening in the Muslim world — particularly in Syria and Egypt — is terrifying to the Israelis. It is a risk they won't live with if they don't have to. So the Israelis switched their policy in Georgia with lightning speed. This could create

145

frictions with the United States, but the Israeli-American relationship isn't what it used to be.

CHAPTER 6: A Giant Sucking Sound

Hopes Meet Reality
May 20, 2008

In geopolitics, we are frequently confronted with what appears to be a great deal of movement. Sometimes it is the current geopolitical reality breaking apart and a new one emerging. Sometimes it is simply meaningless motion in a fixed geopolitical reality — nothing more than the illusion of movement generated for political reasons as players maneuver within a fixed framework for minor advantage or internal political reasons. In other words, we need to distinguish between geopolitics and politics.

Nowhere is that more important than in the Middle East, which increasingly has come to be defined in terms of the Arab-Israeli equation for reasons we don't fully understand. Leaving that aside, in recent months we have been chronicling endless happenings and rumors of happenings, trying to figure out whether the region's geopolitics were redefining themselves or whether we were simply seeing movement within the old paradigm.

In the past few weeks, the noise has intensified, reaching a crescendo with U.S. President George W. Bush's visit to the region. There were four axes of activity:

- Talk about a deal between Israel and the Palestinians.
- Talk about a deal between the Syrians and Israelis.
- Fighting in Lebanon between Hezbollah and its enemies.
- Israeli Prime Minister Ehud Olmert under investigation for taking bribes.

Taken together, it would seem something is likely to happen. We need to examine whether something — and if so, what — is likely to happen.

Talk of an Israeli-Palestinian Deal

Let's begin with the talk of a deal between the Israelis and Palestinians and with the fact that this description is a misnomer. The Palestinians are split geographically between the West Bank and the Gaza Strip and ideologically into two very distinct groups. The West Bank is controlled by the Palestinian National Authority (PNA), which as an institution is split between two factions, Fatah and Hamas. Fatah is stronger in the West Bank than in Gaza and controls the institutions of the PNA. It is almost fair to say that the PNA — the official Palestinian government — is in practice an instrument of Fatah and that therefore Fatah controls the West Bank while Hamas controls Gaza.

Ideologically, Fatah is a secular movement, originating in the left-wing Arabism of the 1960s and 1970s.

Hamas is a religiously-driven organization originating from the Sunni religious movements of the late 1980s and 1990s. Apart from being Palestinian and supporting a Palestinian state, it has different and opposed views of what such a state should look like both internally and geographically. Fatah appears prepared to make geographical compromises with Israel to secure a state that follows its ideology. Its flexibility in part comes from its fear that Hamas could supplant it as the dominant force among the Palestinians. For its part, Hamas is not prepared to make a geographical compromise except on a temporary basis. It has made it clear that while it would accept a truce with Israel, it will not accept a permanent peace agreement nor recognize Israel's right to exist.

Israel also is split on the question of a settlement with the Palestinians, but not as profoundly and institutionally as the Palestinians are divided. It is reasonable to say that the Israeli-Palestinian conflict has become a three-way war between Hamas, Fatah and Israel, with Fatah and Israel increasingly allied against Hamas. But that is what makes the possibility of a settlement between Israel and the Palestinians impossible to imagine. There can be a settlement with the PNA, and therefore with Fatah, but Fatah does not in any way speak for Hamas. Even if Palestinian President Mahmoud Abbas could generate support within Fatah for a comprehensive settlement, it would not constitute a settlement with the Palestinians, but rather only with the dominant faction of the Palestinians in the West Bank.

Given the foregoing, the Israelis have been signaling that they are prepared to move into Gaza in an attempt to crush Hamas' leadership. Indeed, they have signaled that they expect to do so. We could dismiss this as psychological warfare, but Hamas expects Israel to move into Gaza and, in some ways, hopes Israel does so that it can draw the Israelis into counterinsurgency operations in an inhospitable environment. This would burnish Hamas' credentials as the real anti-Israeli warriors, undercutting Fatah and the Shiite group Hezbollah in the process.

For Israel, there might be an advantage in reaching a settlement with Abbas and then launching an attack on Gaza. Abbas might himself want to see Israel crush Hamas, but it would put him and the PNA in a difficult position politically if they just stood by and watched. Second, the Israelis are under no illusions that an attack on Gaza would either be easy or even succeed in the mission of crushing Hamas' military capability. The more rockets fired by Hamas against Israel, the more pressure there is in Israel for some sort of action. But here we have a case of swirling activity leading to paralysis. Optimistic talk of a settlement is just talk. There will be no settlement without war, and, in our opinion, war will undermine Fatah's ability to reach a settlement — and a settlement with the PNA would solve little in any event.

Talk of a Syrian-Israeli Peace Agreement

There also is the ongoing discussion of a Syrian-Israeli peace agreement. Turkey is brokering these talks, driven by a desire to see a stable Syria along its border and to become a major power broker in the region. The Turks are slowly increasing their power and influence under the expectation that in due course, as the United States withdraws from Iraq, a power vacuum will exist that Turkey will have to — and want to — fill. Turkish involvement in Syria represents a first step in exercising diplomatic influence to Turkey's south.

Syria has an interest in a settlement with Israel. The al Assad government is composed of an ethnic minority — the Alawites, a heterodox offshoot of Shiite Islam. It is a secular government with ideological roots much closer to Fatah than to Hamas (both religious and Sunni) or Hezbollah (Shiite but religious). It presides over a majority Sunni country, and it has brutally suppressed Sunni religiosity before. At a time when the Saudis, who do not like Syria, are flush with cash and moving with confidence, the al Assad regime has increased concerns about Sunni dissatisfaction. Moreover, its interests are not in Israel, but in Lebanon, where the region's commercial wealth is concentrated.

Syria dabbles in all the muddy waters of the region. It has sent weapons to Sunni jihadists. Hamas' exiled central leadership is in Damascus. It supports Hezbollah in Lebanon. Syria thus rides multiple and incompatible horses in an endless balancing act designed to preserve the al Assad government. The al Assads have been skillful politicians, but in the end, their efforts have been all tactics and no strategy. The Turks, who do not want to see chaos on their southern border, are urging the Syrians to a strategic decision, or more precisely to the status quo ante 2006.

The United States has never trusted the al Assads, but the situation became particularly venomous after the 2003 invasion of Iraq, when the Syrians, for complex political reasons, decided to allow Sunni fundamentalists to transit through Syria into Iraq. The Syrian motive was to inoculate itself against Sunni fundamentalism — which opposed

Damascus — by making itself useful to the Sunni fundamentalists. The United States countered the Syrian move by generating pressure that forced the Syrian army out of Lebanon.

The Israelis and Syrians have had a working understanding on Lebanon ever since the Israeli withdrawal from Lebanon. Under this understanding, the Syrians would be the dominant force in Lebanon, extracting maximum economic advantage while creating a framework for stability. In return, Syria would restrain Hezbollah both from attacks on Israel and from attacks on Syrian allies in Lebanon — which include many groups opposed to Hezbollah.

The Syrian withdrawal was not greeted with joy in Israel. First, the Israelis liked the arrangement, as it secured their frontier with Lebanon. Second, the Israelis did not want anything to happen to the al Assad regime. Anything that would replace the al Assads would, in the Israeli mind, be much worse. Israel, along with the al Assads, did not want regime change in Damascus and did not want chaos in Lebanon but did want Hezbollah to be controlled by someone other than Israel. And this was a point of tension between Israel and the United States, which was prepared to punish the al Assads for their interference in Iraq — even if the successor Syrian regime would be composed of the Sunni fundamentalists the Syrians had aided.

The Turkish argument is basically that the arrangement between Syria and Lebanon prior to 2006 was in the best interests of Israel and Syria, but that its weakness was that it was informal. Unlike the Israeli-Egyptian or Israeli-Jordanian agreements, which have been stable realities in the region, the Israeli-Syrian relationship was a wink and a nod that could not stand up under U.S. pressure. Turkey has therefore been working to restore the pre-2006 reality, this time formally.

Two entities clearly oppose this settlement. One is the United States. Another is Hezbollah.

The United States sees Syria as a destabilizing factor in the region, regardless of Syria's history in Lebanon. In addition, as Saudi oil revenues rise and U.S. relations with Sunnis in Iraq improve, the Americans must listen very carefully to the Saudis. As we pointed out, the Saudis view Syria — a view forged during the 1970s — as an enemy. The Saudis also consider the Alawite domination of Syrian Sunnis as unacceptable in the long run. Saudi Arabia is also extremely worried about the long-term power of Hezbollah (and Iran) and does not trust the Syrians to control the Shiite group. More precisely, the Saudis believe the Syrians will constrain Hezbollah against Israel, but not necessarily against Saudi and other Sunni interests. The United States is caught between Israeli interest in a formal deal and Saudi hostility. With its own sympathies running against Syria, the U.S. tendency is to want to gently sink the deal.

In this, U.S. interests ironically are aligned with Hezbollah and, to some extent, Iran. Hezbollah grew prosperous under Syrian domination, but it did not increase its political power. The Syrians kept the Shiite group in a box to be opened in the event of war. Hezbollah does not want to go into that box again. It is enjoying its freedom of action to pursue its own interests independent of Syria. It is in Hezbollah's interests to break the deal. Lacking many allies, the Iranians need the Syrians, as different as the

Syrians are ideologically. Iran is walking a tightrope between Syria and Hezbollah on this. But Tehran, too, would like to sink the talks.

The Bizarre Events in Lebanon

Which leads to the bizarre events in Lebanon. The Lebanese Cabinet demanded that Hezbollah turn its proprietary communications network over to the Lebanese government. The demand amounted to the same thing as asking that Hezbollah go out of business. The Lebanese government did not have anywhere near the power needed to force Hezbollah to acquiesce, nor could the Lebanese have imagined for a moment that Hezbollah would do so voluntarily. Why the Lebanese government made an impossible and unenforceable demand that would inevitably lead Hezbollah to take offensive action is unclear. That it did happen is clear.

One theory is that the Americans encouraged Lebanon to do so to put Hezbollah on the defensive. The problem with that theory is that the only possible outcome of that move was the opposite result. Another explanation is that Syria got the Cabinet to do this to justify Syrian intervention against Hezbollah as part of the Syrian-Israeli-Turkish talks. The problem with that theory is that such intervention didn't happen, and Lebanese Prime Minister Fouad Siniora is not a naive man. He likes commitments up front and in blood.

The other explanation is that Siniora knew perfectly well that Hezbollah would go ballistic and he wanted Hezbollah to do so. The Christians, Druze and Sunnis of

Lebanon do not like Hezbollah, but many see Syrian domination of Lebanon as far worse. By increasing Hezbollah's power and increasing the complexity and danger of Lebanon, Siniora wanted to increase the cost of Syrian intervention and increase the strength of those in Damascus who don't want a deal with Israel. It is one thing for Syria to walk into a wide-open country. It is another for Syria to walk into a civil war that the Israelis wouldn't touch. Under this theory, Siniora's move was the Lebanese strategy for preserving its independence from Syria. The move might not work, but you work with what you have.

In all of this, Israeli Prime Minister Ehud Olmert is under investigation for accepting bribes. His defense is that he took the money but didn't do anything in return. The whispers he is generating are that the entire investigation is an attempt by political opponents to discredit him. His opponents are whispering with equal intensity that the money he took is merely the tip of an iceberg of money from outside Israel — primarily from American Jews seeking to have their path into Israeli investments smoothed by Olmert.

Whatever the truth, Israel is in a massive political crisis, with no clear and popular successor to Olmert. This reality further undermines the probability that any decisive strategic settlements will emerge. For Israel to reach agreements with Fatah or Syria, to manage its interests in Lebanon and to manage its relations with the United States, it needs, if not political consensus, at least not political chaos. And political chaos is what Israel has at this moment, as everyone waits to see what actually comes of the investigations. For a merely political event, such chaos could not have come at a more strategic moment.

Geopolitics is being sucked into politics, and apparent breakthroughs are being turned into routine nonevents. The Israeli-Palestinian talks are being sucked into Palestinian politics. The Syrian-Israeli talks are being sucked into Lebanese politics and the complexities of American regional politics. The entire package of opportunities is being sucked into internal Israeli politics.

In the Middle East, apparent geopolitical opportunities are continually undermined by political realities. Or to put it a different way, the geopolitical opportunities are illusory and the real geopolitics of the region are intractable. We still see the Israeli-Syrian relationship as the most promising in the mess. But whether it can rise to the level of a formal agreement is dubious indeed.

Hamas and the Arab States
Jan. 7, 2009

Israel is now in the 12th day of carrying out Operation Cast Lead against the Palestinian Islamist movement Hamas in the Gaza Strip, where Hamas has been the de facto ruler ever since it seized control of the territory in a June 2007 coup. The Israeli campaign, whose primary military aim is to neutralize Hamas' ability to carry out rocket attacks against Israel, has led to the reported deaths of more than 560 Palestinians; the number of wounded is approaching the 3,000 mark.

The reaction from the Arab world has been mixed. On the one hand, a look at the so-called Arab street will reveal an angry scene of chanting protesters, burning flags and embassy attacks in protest of Israel's actions. The principal Arab regimes, however, have either kept quiet or publicly condemned Hamas for the crisis — while privately and frequently expressing their support for Israel's bid to weaken the radical Palestinian group.

Despite the much-hyped Arab nationalist solidarity often cited in the name of Palestine, most Arab regimes actually have little love for the Palestinians. While these countries like keeping the Palestinian issue alive for domestic consumption and as a tool to pressure Israel and the West when the need arises, in actuality they tend to view Palestinian refugees — and Palestinian radical groups like Hamas — as a threat to the stability of their regimes.

One such Arab country is Saudi Arabia. Given its financial power and its shared religious underpinnings with Hamas, Riyadh traditionally has backed the radical Palestinian group. The kingdom backed a variety of Islamist political forces during the 1960s and 1970s in a bid to undercut secular Nasserite Arab nationalist forces, which threatened Saudi Arabia's regional status. But 9/11, which stemmed in part from Saudi support for the Taliban and al Qaeda in Afghanistan, opened Riyadh's eyes to the danger of supporting militant Islamism.

Thus, while Saudi Arabia continued to support many of the same Palestinian groups, it also started whistling a more moderate tune in its domestic and foreign policies. As part of this moderate drive, in 2002 King Abdullah offered Israel a comprehensive peace treaty whereby Arab states would normalize ties with the Jewish state in exchange for an Israeli withdrawal to its 1967 borders. Though Israel rejected the offer, the proposal itself clearly conflicted with Hamas' manifesto, which calls for Israel's destruction. The post-9/11 world also created new problems for one of Hamas' sources of regular funding — wealthy Gulf Arabs — who grew increasingly wary of turning up on the radars of Western security and intelligence agencies as fund transfers from the Gulf came under closer scrutiny.

Meanwhile, Egypt, which regularly mediates Hamas-Israel and Hamas-Fatah matters, thus far has been the most vocal in its opposition to Hamas during the latest Israeli military offensive. Cairo has even gone as far as blaming Hamas for provoking the conflict. Though Egypt's stance has earned it a number of attacks on its embassies in the Arab world and condemnations in major Arab editorial pages, Cairo has a core strategic interest in ensuring that Hamas remains boxed in. The secular government of Egyptian President Hosni Mubarak is already preparing for a shaky leadership transition, which is bound to be exploited by the country's largest opposition movement, the Muslim Brotherhood.

The Muslim Brotherhood, from which Hamas emerged, maintains links with the Hamas leadership. Egypt's powerful security apparatus has kept the group in check, but the Egyptian group has steadily built up support among Egypt's lower and middle classes, which have grown disillusioned with the soaring rate of unemployment and lack of economic prospects in Egypt. The sight of Muslim Brotherhood activists leading protests in Egypt in the name of Hamas is thus quite disconcerting for the Mubarak regime. The Egyptians also are fearful that Gaza could become a haven for Salafist jihadist groups that could collaborate with Egypt's own jihadist node the longer Gaza remains in disarray under Hamas rule.

Of the Arab states, Jordan has the most to lose from a group like Hamas. More than three-fourths of the Hashemite monarchy's people claim Palestinian origins. The kingdom itself is a weak, poor state that historically has relied on the United Kingdom, Israel and the United States for its survival. Among all Arab governments, Amman has had the longest and closest relationship with Israel — even before it concluded a formal peace treaty with Israel in 1994. In 1970, Jordan waged war against Fatah when the group posed a threat to the kingdom's security; it also threw out Hamas in 1999 after fears that the group posed a similar threat to the stability of the kingdom. Like Egypt, Jordan also has a vibrant Muslim Brotherhood, which has closer ties to Hamas than its Egyptian counterpart. As far as Amman is concerned, therefore, the harder Israel hits Hamas, the better.

Finally, Syria is in a more complex position than these other four Arab states. The Alawite-Baathist regime in Syria has long been a pariah in the Arab world because of its support for Shiite Iran and for its mutual militant proxy in Lebanon, Hezbollah. But ever since the 2006 war between Israel and Hezbollah, the Syrians have been charting a different course, looking for ways to break free from diplomatic isolation and to reach some sort of understanding with the Israelis.

For the Syrians, support for Hamas, Palestinian Islamic Jihad and several other radical Palestinian outfits provides tools of leverage to use in negotiating a settlement with Israel. Any deal between the Syrians and the Israelis would thus involve Damascus sacrificing militant proxies such as Hezbollah and Hamas in return for key concessions in Lebanon — where Syria's core geopolitical interests lie — and in the disputed Golan Heights. While the Israeli-Syrian peace talks remain in flux, Syria's lukewarm reaction to the Israeli offensive and restraint (thus far) from criticizing the more moderate Arab regimes' lack of response suggests Damascus may be looking to exploit the Gaza offensive to improve its relations in the Arab world and reinvigorate its talks with Israel. And the more damage Israel does to Hamas now, the easier it will be for Damascus to crack down on Hamas should the need arise.

With Saudi Arabia, Egypt, Jordan and Syria taking into account their own interests when dealing with the Palestinians, ironically, the most reliable patron Sunni Hamas has had in recent years is Iran, the Sunni Arab world's principal Shiite rival. Several key developments have made Hamas' gradual shift toward Iran possible:

- Saudi Arabia's post-9/11 move into the moderate camp — previously dominated by Egypt and Jordan, two states that have diplomatic relations with Israel.

- The collapse of Baathist Iraq and the resulting rise of Shiite power in the region.

- The 2004 Iranian parliamentary elections that put Iran's ultraconservatives in power and the 2005 election of President Mahmoud Ahmadinejad, whose public anti-Israeli views resonated with Hamas at a time when other Arab states had grown more moderate.

- The 2006 Palestinian elections, in which Hamas defeated its secular rival, Fatah, by a landslide. When endowed with the responsibility of running an unrecognized government, Hamas foundered between its goals of dominating the Palestinian political landscape and continuing to call for the destruction of Israel and the creation of an Islamist state. The Arab states, particularly Saudi Arabia and Egypt, had hoped that the electoral victory would lead Hamas to moderate its stance, but Iran encouraged Hamas to adhere to its radical agenda. As the West increasingly isolated the Hamas-led government, the group shifted more toward the Iranian position, which more closely meshed with its original mandate.

- The 2006 summer military confrontation between Hezbollah and Israel, in which Iranian-backed Hezbollah symbolically defeated the Jewish state. Hezbollah's ability to withstand the Israeli military onslaught gave confidence to Hamas that it could emulate the Lebanese Shiite movement — which, like Hamas, was both a political party and an armed paramilitary organization. Similar to their reaction to the current Gaza offensive, the principal Arab states condemned Hezbollah for provoking Israel and grew terrified at the outpouring of support for the Shiite militant group from their own populations. Hezbollah-Hamas collaboration in training, arms-procurement and funding intensified, and almost certainly has played a decisive role in equipping Hamas with 122mm BM-21 Grad artillery rockets and larger Iranian-made 240mm Fajr-3 rockets — and potentially even a modest anti-armor capability.

- The June 2007 Hamas coup against Fatah in the Gaza Strip, which caused a serious strain in relations between Egypt and Hamas. The resulting blockade on Gaza put Egypt in an extremely uncomfortable position, in which it had to crack down on the Gaza border, thus giving the Muslim Brotherhood an excuse to rally opposition against Cairo. Egypt was already uncomfortable with Hamas' electoral victory, but it could not tolerate the group's emergence as the unchallenged power in Gaza.

- Syria's decision to go public with peace talks with Israel. As soon as it became clear that Syria was getting serious about such negotiations, alarm bells went off within groups like Hamas and Hezbollah, which now had to deal with the fear that Damascus could sell them out at any time as part of a deal with the Israelis.

Hamas' relations with the Arab states already were souring; its warming relationship with Iran has proved the coup de grace. Mubarak said it best when he recently remarked that the situation in the Gaza Strip "has led to Egypt, in practice, having a border with Iran." In other words, Hamas has allowed Iranian influence to come far too close for the Arab states' comfort.

In many ways, the falling-out between Hamas and the Arab regimes is not surprising. The decline of Nasserism in the late 1960s essentially meant the death of Arab nationalism. Even before then, the Arab states put their respective national interests ahead of any devotion to pan-Arab nationalism that would have translated into support for the Palestinian cause. As Islamism gradually came to replace Arab nationalism as a political force throughout the region, the Arab regimes became even more concerned about stability at home, given the very real threat of a religious challenge to their rule. While these states worked to suppress radical Islamist elements that had taken root in their countries, the Arab governments caught wind of Tehran's attempts to adopt the region's radical Islamist trend to create a geopolitical space for Iran in the Arab Middle East. As a result, the Arab-Persian struggle became one of the key drivers that has turned the Arab states against Hamas.

For each of these Arab states, Hamas represents a force that could stir the social pot at home — either by creating a backlash against the regimes for their ties to Israel and their perceived failure to aid the Palestinians, or by emboldening democratic Islamist movements in the region that could threaten the stability of both republican regimes and monarchies. With somewhat limited options to contain Iranian expansion in the region, the Arab states ironically are looking to Israel to ensure that Hamas remains boxed in. So, while on the surface it may seem that the entire Arab world is convulsing with anger at Israel's offensive against Hamas, a closer look reveals that the view from the Arab palace is quite different from the view on the Arab street.

An Israeli Prime Minister Goes to Washington
May 18, 2009

Israeli Prime Minister Benjamin Netanyahu is visiting Washington for his first official visit with U.S. President Barack Obama. A range of issues — including the future of Israeli-Palestinian negotiations, Israeli-Syrian talks and Iran policy — are on the table. This is one of an endless series of meetings between U.S. presidents and Israeli prime ministers over the years, many of which concerned these same issues. Yet little has changed.

That Israel has a new prime minister and the United States a new president might appear to make this meeting significant. But this is Netanyahu's second time as prime minister, and his government is as diverse and fractious as most recent Israeli governments. Israeli politics are in gridlock, with deep divisions along multiple fault lines and an electoral system designed to magnify disagreements.

Obama is much stronger politically, but he has consistently acted with caution, particularly in the foreign policy arena. Much of his foreign policy follows from the Bush administration. He has made no major breaks in foreign policy beyond rhetoric; his policies on Iraq, Afghanistan, Iran, Russia and Europe are essentially extensions of pre-existing policy. Obama faces major economic problems in the United States and clearly is not looking for major changes in foreign policy. He understands how quickly public sentiment can change, and he does not plan to take risks he does not have to take right now.

This, then, is the problem: Netanyahu is coming to Washington hoping to get Obama to agree to fundamental redefinitions of the regional dynamic. For example, he wants Obama to re-examine the commitment to a two-state solution in the Israeli-Palestinian dispute. (Netanyahu's foreign minister, Avigdor Lieberman, has said Israel is no longer bound by prior commitments to that concept.) Netanyahu also wants the United States to commit itself to a finite time frame for talks with Iran, after which unspecified but ominous-sounding actions are to be taken.

Facing a major test in Afghanistan and Pakistan, Obama has more than enough to deal with at the moment. Moreover, U.S. presidents who get involved in Israeli-Palestinian negotiations frequently get sucked into a morass from which they do not return. For Netanyahu to even request that the White House devote attention to the Israeli-Palestinian problem at present is asking a lot. Asking for a complete review of the peace process is even less realistic.

Obstacles to the Two-State Solution

The foundation of the Israeli-Palestinian peace process for years has been the assumption that there would be a two-state solution. Such a solution has not materialized for a host of reasons. First, at present there are two Palestinian entities, Gaza and the West Bank, which are hostile to each other. Second, the geography and economy of any Palestinian state would be so reliant on Israel that independence would be meaningless; geography simply makes the two-state proposal almost impossible to implement. Third, no Palestinian government would have the power to guarantee that rogue elements would not launch rockets at Israel, potentially striking at the Tel Aviv-Jerusalem corridor, Israel's heartland. And fourth, neither the Palestinians nor the Israelis have the domestic political coherence to allow any negotiator to operate from a position of confidence. Whatever the two sides negotiated would be revised and destroyed by their political opponents, and even their friends.

For this reason, the entire peace process — including the two-state solution — is a chimera. Neither side can live with what the other can offer. But if it is a fiction, it is a fiction that serves U.S. purposes. The United States has interests that go well beyond Israeli interests and sometimes go in a different direction altogether. Like Israel, the United States understands that one of the major obstacles to any serious evolution toward a two-state solution is Arab hostility to such an outcome.

The Jordanians have feared and loathed Fatah in the West Bank ever since the Black September uprisings of 1970. The ruling Hashemites are ethnically different from the Palestinians (who constitute an overwhelming majority of the Jordanian population), and they fear that a Palestinian state under Fatah would threaten the Jordanian monarchy. For their part, the Egyptians see Hamas as a descendent of the Muslim Brotherhood, which seeks the Mubarak government's ouster — meaning Cairo would hate to see a Hamas-led state. Meanwhile, the Saudis and the other Arab states do not wish to see a radical altering of the status quo, which would likely come about with the rise of a Palestinian polity.

At the same time, whatever the basic strategic interests of the Arab regimes, all pay lip service to the principle of Palestinian statehood. This is hardly a unique situation. States frequently claim to favor various things they actually are either indifferent to or have no intention of doing anything about. Complicating matters for the Arab states is the fact that they have substantial populations that do care about the fate of the Palestinians. These states thus are caught between public passion on behalf of Palestinians and the regimes' interests that are threatened by the Palestinian cause. The states' challenge, accordingly, is to appear to be doing something on behalf of the Palestinians while in fact doing nothing.

The United States has a vested interest in the preservation of these states. The futures of Egypt, Saudi Arabia and the Gulf states are of vital importance to Washington. The United States must therefore publicly demonstrate its sensitivity to pressures from these nations over the Palestinian question while being careful to achieve nothing — an easy enough goal to achieve.

The various Israeli-Palestinian peace processes have thus served U.S. and Arab interests quite well. They provide the illusion of activity, with high-level visits breathlessly reported in the media, succeeded by talks and concessions — all followed by stalemate and new rounds of violence, thus beginning the cycle all over again.

The Palestinian Peace Process as Political Theater

One of the most important proposals Netanyahu is bringing to Obama calls for reshaping the peace process. If Israeli President Shimon Peres is to be believed, Netanyahu will not back away from the two-state formula. Instead, the Israeli prime minister is asking that the various Arab-state stakeholders become directly involved in the negotiations. In other words, Netanyahu is proposing that Arab states with very different public and private positions on Palestinian statehood be asked to participate — thereby forcing them to reveal publicly their true positions, ultimately creating internal political crises in the Arab states.

The clever thing about this position is that Netanyahu not only knows his request will not become a reality, but he also does not want it to become a reality. The political stability of Jordan, Saudi Arabia and Egypt is as much an Israeli interest as an American one. Indeed, Israel even wants a stable Syria, since whatever would come after the Alawite regime in Damascus would be much more dangerous to Israeli security than the current Syrian regime.

Overall, Israel is a conservative power. In terms of nation-states, it does not want upheaval; it is quite content with the current regimes in the Arab world. But Netanyahu would love to see an international conference with the Arab states roundly condemning Israel publicly. This would shore up the justification for Netanyahu's policies domestically while simultaneously creating a framework for reshaping world opinion by showing an Israel isolated among hostile states.

Obama is likely hearing through diplomatic channels from the Arab countries that they do not want to participate directly in the Palestinian peace process. And the United States really does not want them there, either. The peace process normally ends in a train wreck anyway, and Obama is in no hurry to see the wreckage. He will want to insulate other allies from the fallout, putting off the denouement of the peace process as long as possible. Obama has sent George Mitchell as his Middle East special envoy to deal with the issue, and from the U.S. president's point of view, that is quite enough attention to the problem.

Netanyahu, of course, knows all this. Part of his mission is simply convincing his ruling coalition — and particularly Lieberman, whom Netanyahu needs to survive, and who is by far Israel's most aggressive foreign minister ever — that he is committed to redefining the entire Israeli-Palestinian relationship. But in a broader context, Netanyahu is looking for greater freedom of action. By posing a demand the United States will not grant, Israel is positioning itself to ask for something that appears smaller.

Israel and the Appearance of Freedom of Action

What Israel actually would do with greater freedom of action is far less important than simply creating the appearance that the United States has endorsed Israel's ability to act in a new and unpredictable manner. From Israel's point of view, the problem with Israeli-Palestinian relations is that Israel is under severe constraints from the United States, and the Palestinians know it. This means that the Palestinians can even anticipate the application of force by Israel, meaning they can prepare for it and endure it. From Netanyahu's point of view, Israel's primary problem is that the Palestinians are confident they know what the Israelis will do. If Netanyahu can get Obama to introduce a degree of ambiguity into the situation, Israel could regain the advantage of uncertainty.

The problem for Netanyahu is that Washington is not interested in having anything unpredictable happen in Israeli-Palestinian relations. The United States is quite content with the current situation, particularly while Iraq becomes more stable and the Afghan situation remains unstable. Obama does not want a crisis from the Mediterranean to the Hindu Kush. The fact that Netanyahu has a political coalition to satisfy will not interest the United States, and while Washington at some unspecified point might endorse a peace conference, it will not be until Israel and its foreign minister endorse the two-state formula.

Netanyahu will then shift to another area where freedom of action is relevant — namely, Iran. The Israelis have leaked to the Israeli media that the Obama administration has told them that Israel may not attack Iran without U.S. permission, and that Israel agreed to this requirement. (U.S. President George W. Bush and Israeli Prime Minister Ehud Olmert went through the same routine not too long ago, using a good cop/bad cop act in a bid to kick-start negotiations with Iran.)

In reality, Israel would have a great deal of difficulty attacking Iranian facilities with non-nuclear forces. A multitarget campaign 1,000 miles away against an enemy with some air defenses could be a long and complex operation. Such a raid would require a long trip through U.S.-controlled airspace for the fairly small Israeli air force.

Israel could use cruise missiles, but the tonnage of high explosive delivered by a cruise missile cannot penetrate even moderately hardened structures; the same is true for ICBMs carrying conventional warheads. Israel would have to notify the United States of its intentions because it would be passing through Iraqi airspace — and because U.S. technical intelligence would know what it was up to before Israeli aircraft even took off. The idea that Israel might consider attacking Iran without informing Washington is therefore absurd on the surface. Even so, the story has surfaced yet again in an Israeli newspaper in a virtual carbon copy of stories published more than a year ago.

Netanyahu has promised that the endless stalemate with the Palestinians will not be allowed to continue. He also knows that whatever happens, Israel cannot threaten the stability of Arab states that are by and large uninterested in the Palestinians. He also understands that in the long run, Israel's freedom of action is defined by the United States, not by Israel. His electoral platform and his strategic realities have never aligned. Arguably, it might be in the Israeli interest that the status quo be disrupted, but it is not in the American interest. Netanyahu therefore will get to redefine neither the Palestinian situation nor the Iranian situation. Israel simply lacks the power to impose the reality it wants, the current constellation of Arab regimes it needs, and the strategic relationship with the United States on which Israeli national security rests.

In the end, this is a classic study in the limits of power. Israel can have its freedom of action anytime it is willing to pay the price for it. But Israel can't pay the price. Netanyahu is coming to Washington to see if he can get what he wants without paying the price, and we suspect strongly he knows he won't get it. His problem is the same as that of the Arab states. There are many in Israel, particularly among Netanyahu's supporters, who believe Israel is a great power. It isn't. It is a nation that is strong partly because it lives in a pretty weak neighborhood, and partly because it has very strong friends. Many Israelis don't want to be told that, and Netanyahu came to office playing on the sense of Israeli national power.

So the peace process will continue, no one will expect anything from it, the Palestinians will remain isolated and wars regularly will break out. The only advantage of this situation from the U.S. point of view is that it is preferable to all other available realities.

Made in the USA
Charleston, SC
24 February 2011